MICHAEL KEATING is Professor of Politics at the University of Aberdeen, part-time Professor at the University of Edinburgh and Director of the ESRC Centre on Constitutional Change. He has a BA from the University of Oxford and in 1975 Caledonian University. He Western Ontario and the Spain and France. He is ny, the Royal Society of Keating is the author or politics, nationalism and ce of Scotland (Oxford te (Oxford University

ity of Aberdeen and m the University of h and his PhD was Aberdeen, Stirling politics and nation- including Better user (@MalcH). conomic Review

Luath Press is an independently owned and managed book publishing company based in Scotland, and is not aligned to any political party or grouping. *Viewpoints* is an occasional series exploring issues of current and future relevance.

Small Nations in
a Big World

What Scotland can learn

MICHAEL KEATING and MALCOLM HARVEY

Luath Press Limited

EDINBURGH

www.luath.co.uk

First published 2014
Reprinted 2014
New Edition 2015

ISBN: 978-1-910021-77-4

The paper used in this book is recyclable. It is made from
low chlorine pulps produced in a low energy, low emissions manner
from renewable forests.

Printed and bound by
Bell & Bain Ltd., Glasgow

Typeset in 11 point Sabon
by 3btype.com

Contents

List of Figures

List of Tables

Preface and Acknowledgements
to 2015 Edition

THE WORK ON which this book is based was supported by a Senior Fellowship awarded by the Economic and Social Research Programme under its Future of the UK and Scotland programme. It has benefited greatly from discussions with colleagues on the programme. We are grateful to academic colleagues in our case-study countries for advice and ideas. In Denmark, Peter Thisted Dinesen, Ulrik Pram Gad, Bent Greve, Sara Dybris McQuaid and Peter Nedergaard. In Estonia, Kairit Kall, Anu Toots and Karsten Staehr. In Ireland, Frank Barry, John Coakley, Tom Garvin, John Geary, Niamh Hardiman, Rory O'Donnell, Joe Ruane, Jennifer Todd and Christopher Whelan. In Latvia, Jānis Ikstens, Feliciana Rajevska and Liga Rasnaca. In Lithuania, Jonas Čičinskas, Liutauras Gudžinskas, Vytautas Kuokštis and Ramūnas Vilpišauskas. In Norway, Elin Haugsjerd Allern, Harald Baldersheim, Nic Brandal, Øivind Bratberg, Tore Hansen, Ottar Hellevik, Axel West Pedersen and Dag Einar Thorsen. And in Sweden, Carl Dahlström, Jonas Hinnfors Jon Pierre and Bo Rothstein.

Officials in government and civil society have helped us with ideas, reflections and experiences. As they were interviewed off the record, they must remain anonymous, but we are grateful.

Our research has continued under the auspices of the ESRC Centre on Constitutional Change, with its interdisciplinary programme on the future of Scotland. A central theme of this programme is that Scotland's constitutional future concerns not a simple binary choice but rather a whole spectrum of options, including complete independence, the form of attenuated independence with a currency union that was proposed in 2014 and several variants of devolution-max and the status quo. In the aftermath of the referendum, this is more evident than ever. Scotland is still a small nation in a big world, embedded in a complex web of interdependencies in the United Kingdom, the European Union and global markets. Most of the key questions raised in the referendum debate about Scotland's ability to forge its own economic and social project remain as relevant as ever as we debate now powers in taxation and welfare, and Scotland's place in the world.

CHAPTER I

Introduction

IN SEPTEMBER 2014, Scots voted on independence. The question on the ballot was, in appearance, simple and clear: *Should Scotland be an independent country?* Yet, while the words may be admirably concise, the deeper meaning and implications are not. For 'black letter' lawyers, independence is something that a country does or does not have. With independence, it can pass its own laws and is in control of its own destiny. Some of this comes across in the Scottish Government's (2013) white paper on independence, which several times makes the point that: 'Independence means that Scotland's future will be in our own hands.' Yet being formally independent does not mean that a nation is fully in command of its own destiny. In the 1950s, former home rule enthusiast, and wartime Secretary of State for Scotland, Tom Johnston remarked:

> For many years past, I have become, and increasingly become, uneasy lest we should get political power without our first having, or at least simultaneously having, an adequate economy to administer. What purport would there be in getting a Scots Parliament in Edinburgh if it has to administer an emigration system, a glorified Poor Law and a graveyard.
>
> JOHNSTON, 1952: 33

These dilemmas are even more acute in today's globalised world, where nations may gain independence but power always seems to be somewhere else – in the European Union, NATO, the World Trade Organisation, with big corporations or in the anonymous discipline of the market. Yet there are examples of small nations doing very well in global conditions, adapting to external constraints while not being imprisoned by them. Indeed, small countries might even have advantages over their larger neighbours.

At one time, the Scottish National Party (SNP) was so convinced of the virtues of small northern European states that it coined the phrase 'arc of prosperity' to describe them. With the financial crash of 2008 and its devastating effects in Ireland and Iceland, unionists turned the example on its head, talking of the 'arc of insolvency'. Both metaphors were profoundly misleading. Small northern European states have adapted to global pressures in very different ways. Some of them were hit hard by the crisis while others came through it rather well. It is not being small that makes the difference but the way in which a country copes with it. In this book we explore the different ways in which small states adapt and draw some lessons for Scotland.

During much of the 20th century, large states seemed to represent the future, as we show in Chapter 2. They could command large resources, look after themselves in the world and secure big markets and economies of scale. Changes in the world economy and the rise of transnational bodies like the European Union, the World Trade Organisation and NATO, however, have eroded some of the advantages of large states, since they can provide the security and market access that small states need. In a turbulent world, small states might be more flexible, with shorter lines of communication and able to adapt more easily, an argument we examine in Chapter 3. This is not, as some recent contributions would have it, because they are ethnically homogeneous or because everyone in them shares the same policy preferences. A nation is not an ethnic bloc but a political community, in which social and economic compromises can be worked out and common interests brokered.

It is not true, as some prophets of globalisation have proclaimed, that there is only one way of adapting to the changing world. On the contrary, small states have adopted a variety of strategies, as we show in Chapter 4. For the sake of clarifying the argument, we identify two key strategies for adapting to the changing world. The market liberal strategy involves accepting the logic of global markets and seeking to become more competitive by cutting back on the state, bringing down taxes on firms and wealthy individuals, and deregulating labour and product markets. In this way, investment will flow in and prosperity will be secured. This might work in some ways in an underdeveloped economy desperate for inward investment. In a developed welfare state, on the other hand, it implies cutting back on social provision, since you simply cannot cut taxes and maintain services at the same time. Such cuts can not only be socially damaging but might even undermine the public goods such as education, on which the productive economy depends. The alternative strategy is the social investment state, in which public expenditure is seen as a contribution to the productive economy rather than a drain on it. The inescapable corollary of this approach is that taxes will be higher.

The social investment approach has a lot of appeal in Scotland. There are references to it in the independence white paper, and it underlies much of the work of the Jimmy Reid Foundation's (2013) Common Weal, trades unions (STUC, 2012) and the voluntary sector (SCVO, 2013). There are, however, different varieties of it, which may be more, or less, egalitarian and social democratic. None of them should be seen simply as policies that governments can adopt at will but depend for their realisation on the right institutions, an issue we explore in Chapter 5. Many small European countries have used forms of social partnership to get both sides of industry and other groups on board, negotiating key deals and thinking in the long term. Governments need to be more innovative and adaptive, and also need to think for the long term.

Chapters 6, 7 and 8 examine the contrasting experiences of the Nordic countries (close to the social investment state) and the Baltic states (closer to the market liberal model), and of Ireland, which has attempted a hybrid of the two. The lesson is that it is difficult to pick and choose, or to combine, elements of different models at will, since each has its own logic.

Chapter 9 asks whether Scotland has the preconditions for the social investment approach. The answer is mixed. Scottish policy making is characterised by the engagement of groups and government has sought to make itself more strategic, but Scotland lacks the broad social partnership that characterises many successful small states. So external change in the form of independence would need to be matched by considerable internal change before it is fully equipped to face global challenges. There is a broad commitment to the social investment model in its social democratic variant, but a reluctance to pay for it. These questions were not fully addressed in the referendum campaign. The No side systematically portrayed every aspect of independence as negative, while the Yes side sought to avoid choosing between different models of political economy, trying to combine market liberal and social democratic modes.

The work on which this book is based was supported by a Senior Fellowship awarded by the Economic and Social Research Programme under its Future of the UK and Scotland programme. Our work on Scotland's constitutional future continues with ESRC support in the Centre on Constitutional Change.

CHAPTER 2

The Size of States

The Time of Big States

THERE HAS BEEN A transformation of thinking about the size of states over recent decades. During most of the 19th and 20th centuries, mainstream social scientists and historians tended to believe that the large, consolidated nation-state was both good for economic, social and cultural progress and historically inevitable. Arguments about moral worth, economic efficiency and solidarity were piled upon each other to praise the big and condemn the small. In the 21st century, there is altogether less certainty. The nation-state is itself in question, pressured from two sides. Power drifts up to international and supranational institutions, notably the European Union, which is not quite a state but more than an international organisation, and downwards to local and regional levels. Small states have not disappeared but have proven resilient and are often doing rather well. Into this changing geography of power have stepped nationalist movements in Europe's 'stateless nations', making their own claims for self-government, which may or may not entail setting up new states. This has provoked some reflection on the size of nations and states in the emerging, complex and multilevel Europe.

The Moral Worth of Nations

Nobody can suppose that it is not more beneficial for a Breton or a Basque of French Navarre… to be a member of the French nationality, admitted on equal terms to all the privileges of French citizenship… than to sulk on his own rocks, the half-savage relic of past times, revolving in his own little mental orbit, without participation or interest in the general movement of the world. The same remark applies to the Welshman or the Scottish Highlander as members of the British nation.

JOHN STUART MILL (1972), *On Liberty*

There is no country in Europe which does not have in some corner or other one or several ruined fragments of peoples (*Völkerruinen*), the remnant of a former population that was suppressed and held in bondage by the nation which later became the main vehicle of historical development. These relics of a nation mercilessly trampled under foot in the course of history, as Hegel says, these residual fragments of peoples (*Völkerabfälle*) always become fanatical standard-bearers of counter-revolution and remain so until their complete extirpation or loss of their national character, just as their whole existence in general is itself a protest against a great historical revolution.

FRIEDRICH ENGELS (1849), 'The Magyar Struggle'

These two quotations, from the liberal Mill and the Marxist Engels, sum up received wisdom about the size of states in the 19th century and into the 20th. Large states were seen as an inextricable part of the project of modernity and, as they were created and consolidated in the latter part of the century, were the shape of the future. Germany, forged in 1870 from a plethora of small territories under the leadership of Prussia, rapidly powered ahead economically. Italy, united at the same time, saw rapid industrialisation (at least in the north) although its great power pretensions were never to be realised. France, its centralised and homogenised state reinforced during the Third Republic, remained a beacon for other European nation-builders. There were, to be sure, counter-movements in Spain (Catalonia, the Basque Country) and the United Kingdom (Ireland) but much liberal opinion, together with historians, tended, with Mill and Engels, to regard these as relics of a past age, as last stands against modernity.

Liberals might make exception for liberation movements within the great empires of the Habsburgs and Ottomans but even in their case there was a certain contempt for small polities fragmenting the political space. After the Second World War, they could support anti-colonial nationalist movements, but these were cases apart. From the early 20th century, the term 'Balkanisation' was used pejoratively to describe the proliferation of small states based on ethnic groups and their inability to live together. Sometimes this represented a rejection of nationalism for being divisive and against liberal cosmopolitan. More often, it was used to underpin a distinction between good and bad nationalisms. The nationalism of large states is, according to this reading, a civic one, based on patriotism, civil rights and attachment to institutions, while small-state nationalism is an ethnic one, based on fictive history, blood lines and exclusion. Echoes of this are still found, in the works of the late Marxist historian Eric

Hobsbawm or the sociologist and politician Ralph Daherndorf. The latter remarked that, while localism might be desirable, the nation is something else:

> It is possible to counteract the simultaneous pressures towards individu-alisation and centralisation by a new emphasis on local power. The word 'local' is deliberately chosen. Nations within nations – like Wales, or Quebec, or Catalonia – do not have the same effect. They may contribute to a general sense of belonging, but as a principle of social and political organisation they divide and produce unhelpful rigidities (Dahrendorf, 1995).

More recently, Joseph Weiler (2013) has condemned Catalan nationalists (including Scottish and Basque ones in the general criticism) for their:

> regressive and outmoded nationalist ethos which apparently cannot stomach the discipline of loyalty and solidarity that one would expect it owed to its fellow citizens in Spain? The very demand for independence from Spain, an independence from the need to work out political, social, cultural and economic differences within the Spanish polity, independ-ence from the need to work through and transcend history, disqualifies morally and politically Catalonia and the likes as future Member States of the European Union.

Like their 19th-century predecessors, Dahrendorf and Weiler are confusing quite different arguments. There is a longstanding distinction in studies of nationalism between exclusive or 'ethnic' and inclusive or 'civic' nation-alisms. 'Ethnic' nationalisms appeal to questions of blood and ancestry or very restrictive cultural norms while 'civic' nationalisms are more open as to who belongs to the nation. Like others, Hobsbawm, Dahrendorft and Weiler assume that the nationalisms of big nation-states can be civic while those of small and stateless nations are necessarily ethnic and small-minded. In fact it is often historical accident that has converted some nations but not others into states. Both large and small nationalisms can be narrow and exclusive or broad and inclusive. Indeed there are liberal and illiberal elements within any national project. German large-state nationalism has been associated with some of the greatest crimes in history, but there is also a liberal German national tradition. Weiler's linking of liberal Catalan nationalism to the xenophobia of the Italian Northern League makes no more sense that linking liberal nationalism in France to the Fascist tradition.

At one time it was possible to claim that big states were more progressive because they represented a step towards universalism. This claim was always questionable but has become more difficult to defend in recent decades by the process of transnational integration, notably within the European Union. It is Europe, and beyond that the world, that represents the larger space, while the nation-state stands against universalism. Faced with these challenges, established states have to defend their claims to superiority and articulate them more explicitly, hence the debates in the United Kingdom about the meaning and value of Britishness, and similar debates in other countries. State nationalism thus loses its assumed superiority and finds itself placed on the same moral plane as those of the smaller nations, or indeed of supranational institutions. If we no longer take the established large states for granted, we can ask by what moral principle (as opposed to historical accident) Norway and Portugal are independent states but Scotland and Catalonia are not. After all, Norway was, for hundreds of years, part of Denmark and then Sweden, while Portugal was for sixty years united with the kingdoms of Castile and Aragon, the basis of modern Spain.

As for the moral value of nationalisms, this is wholly unrelated to the size of the nation or whether it has a state or not. Some of them may come out well, others badly. Weiler gives no credit to the fact that Catalan, Scottish, Welsh and Basque nationalisms are more highly committed to Europe than their state counterparts. By contrast, the nationalism of the Italian political party Lega Nord, after a flirtation with Europe, is deeply Eurosceptic. Scottish nationalism is open to immigration while the Lega Nord is xenophobic and one strand of Flemish nationalism is deeply hostile to immigration and multiculturalism. Catalan nationalists have made massive efforts to include incomers into the national community while Basque nationalism has moved from an ethnic exclusiveness, which characterised its early years, to a more civic conception of the nation. British nationalism (and, even more so, English nationalism) is increasingly associated with Euroscepticism and opposition to immigration. In a longer historical perspective, big-state nationalisms have covered the whole spectrum from the ethnic exclusiveness, which was a mark of the German model, to the civic republican tradition in France. Big states have frequently been aggressive and expansionist; some small states have sought to expand their borders; and some small states have been peaceful and content within their own frontiers. Good and bad can be found in all categories.

What is striking about many of the national movements in contemporary western Europe is that, contrary to the views of big-state liberals, they do not depend on ethnic exclusivity or essential difference. In fact, they are based on exactly the same moral premises as large-state nationalism and can be assessed within the same framework. Scottish and British, Catalan and Spanish, (and likewise Quebec and Canadian) nationalisms are all founded on liberal democratic principles. Their point of difference concerns the appropriate framework within which these principles can be realised. Nationalism has turned from questions of ethnic identity to arguments about the best way to achieve social and economic outcomes. This is not to say that emotion or considerations of belonging have disappeared from the debate, but instrumental reasoning does play a larger part. One of the key issues is whether larger or smaller states are more effective.

The Advantages of Being Big

During the 20th century, it was often assumed that large states represented the future because they were functionally more efficient. At a time of expanding industry, it helped to have a large internal market and a wide range of productive activities. Germany, after the elimination of barriers (starting with a customs union and culminating with unification in 1870) was able to catch up to the United Kingdom. France eliminated internal customs after the Revolution, as did Spain in the early 19th century. By the mid-20th century, the United States attracted huge interest and envy as a continental-wide single market. The experience of Italy's integrated market after 1870s, on the other hand, was not so positive and many people have argued that it was a mistake.

When the world trading system collapsed between the two world wars, small states were particularly badly hit, forced back on their own restricted domestic markets. Even in less drastic times, having a large and diversified internal market can help a country to weather 'asymmetrical shocks', that is economic problems affecting one sector or region more than others. It is not uncommon in the United States for some regions to be in recessions while others are booming. Unemployed people can then move to where the jobs are. The large federal budget evens out the impact – as incomes fall in the recession regions, taxes automatically fall as well, and their public expenditure can be maintained by the better-off regions.

It was also argued that larger states could exploit economies of scale. This applies most obviously in overseas representation, where they can afford embassies in most countries of the world. There may also be economies in domestic administration and the same number of ministries and agencies are supported by a larger number of taxpayers. Expensive items like research and development could similarly work better on a larger scale, with the burden spread.

These advantages seemed only to increase after the Second World War, when governments accepted responsibility for economic management including full employment, economic growth, price stability and regional balance. Keynesian macroeconomic management, evening out booms and busts, was best managed at a large scale, with central governments mobilising resources and freely spending money. Keynesianism relies on boosting spending at times of recession but the danger, in a small country, is that the benefit will leak abroad as citizens spend their earnings on imports. Gradually, Keynesian macroeconomic policy was complemented with an active government role in sponsoring 'national champions' in key economic sectors, and engaging in various forms of indicative planning in conjunction with the private sector.

Many states developed regional policies aimed at evening out the balance between booming and ailing parts of the country by diverting investment into the latter. During what the French call the *trente glorieuses années* (30 glorious years) (1945–75) regional policy could even be presented as a positive-sum game in which everyone could win. Poor regions gained investment and jobs, rich regions saw a reduction in congestion and sprawl, and the national economy gained from mobilising idle resources and relieving inflationary pressures. Taxpayers in the wealthy regions could take comfort from the fact that much of the money sent to the poorer areas came back in the form of orders for their goods. So within the Italian national market, a newly-employed worker in Calabria would buy a car made in Turin.

Expansion of the welfare state, looking after its citizens from cradle to grave, in the 20th century also favoured big states. T.H. Marshall (1992), writing after the Second World War, saw this as a third phase of citizenship rights, following from civil rights and then political rights. Welfare rights were rooted in a common political community, which was assumed, without a great deal of analysis, to correspond to the nation-state, which in turn was both an administrative unit and a community of belonging. It seemed logical that large states would be better at welfare as they could mobilise larger resources across large geographical spaces. Most welfare benefits, such as support for the unemployed, families and for the old, were awarded on the same criteria irrespective of local residence, and so they expressed broad solidarity. There were also more explicit mechanisms for transferring resources to local governments on the principle that rich and poor regions should be able to provide the same level of services irrespective of fiscal capacity. If one region was in trouble, it would draw down welfare support while in other times it could be a net contributor. If national solidarity was strong enough, such transfers could even be permanent rather than sporadic, the price paid for national unity. Welfare states were thus a centralising influence and both drew on, and in turn strengthened, a sense of common destiny and solidarity.

Finally, in an uncertain and dangerous world, size seemed to offer a degree of protection against aggression. Only large states could afford large armies, navies and the modern military technology of the late 19th and early 20th century arms races. Small states might rely on international guarantees but these were often swept aside, as happened to Belgium in 1914. The fate of Czechoslovakia in 1938 showed that even their supposed protector could connive in their destruction. Since the Congress of Vienna in 1815 it had been the big powers that disposed of the affairs the continent, including recognition of states, installation of monarchs and any moving of boundaries. Intellectual cover was given to great power pretensions by the geo-politics school of geographers, who believed that nations had destinies determined by their geographical location and strategic interests. Influence stemmed from size, resources and command of land or the seas, while the great powers struggled for supremacy.

Other Histories

In a longer historical perspective, however, this inexorable trend towards larger states is less evident. History has known many different types of polity, to use the neutral term that Ferguson and Mansbach (1996) employ to avoid the loaded connotations of 'state' (Spruyt, 1994). Over much of European space and history the dominant mode of rule has been the empire. We tend to associate this term with the colonial rule practised by western powers in the southern hemisphere in the 19th and 20th centuries, giving it strongly negative connotations. There have, however, been empires within European space, from Roman and Byzantine empires, through the Holy

Roman Empire to the Habsburg, Ottoman (Turkish), Romanov (Russian) and Hohenzollern (German empires), the last three enduring until the First World War. Such empires were not, of course, democracies but then nor, until the 20th century, were nation-states. Some did, however, sustain a degree of cultural and national pluralism that nation-states, with their urge to unity, often could not. History has also seen city-states, autonomous provinces, ecclesiastical jurisdictions and trading associations such as the Hanseatic League.

The viability of various forms of polity has depended, among other things, on wider trading conditions, military technology and the balance of forces among the great powers. In the early modern period (the fifteenth to seventeenth centuries), trading city states such as Venice, Genoa, Rijeka and the Hanseatic cities, along with the provinces and cities of Flanders, could survive and prosper from their position astride trading routes. Catalonia, a trading polity embedded within the confederal Kingdom of Aragon, traded into the Mediterranean, expanding its cultural and political influence at the same time. Some small polities could mobilise their own military power (as shown by the Venetian navy and arsenal) but otherwise troops could be purchased, Switzerland and Scotland being among the main suppliers of mercenaries. Some people have imagined this to be a form of early neo-liberal free-trading market capitalism but in practice these trading ventures were highly regulated and under public control. The Italian trading states were organised around commerce while the Hanse, far from being a free-trade zone, was a cartel.

Other polities survived at the interface between great powers, playing one off against another. Scotland played England against France for centuries and survived as a polity despite the weakness of its monarchy. The Netherlands emerged in the context of war between England and Spain. Stein Rokkan (1999) drew attention to the 'shatter-belt' of territories that maintained their identities between the state-building projects of the great powers. Many of these were located on the trade routes of early modern times; indeed the pattern re-emerged in the 1980 when French economists developed the idea of the 'blue banana' of prosperous regions from Flanders down to northern Italy – so called because of its shape on the map. Still other polities survived at the periphery of the state system, as in Scandinavia, or turned towards global empire, as did Portugal. Some have attributed the demise of these small polities to changing military technology. They could not afford the demands of 18th-century warfare or assemble the masses of troops needed. Certainly by the Napoleonic era they were defenceless as the fate of the Venetian Republic, tossed to the Habsburgs, shows.

Large states were not just the result of changing geo-political, techno-logical and trading patterns but themselves helped to mould those patterns. Big-nation states reshaped trading relations, creating national markets. They dismantled economic barriers within the state but, in the process, broke older trading links and markets and created new economic bound-aries. Some elements of the old order survived, such as the distinctive Basque economic system, which maintained free trade with the rest of the world and customs posts with the rest of Spain, but most countries followed France, which abolished internal customs at the Revolution while setting an economic frontier at the external border. The effect was often to turn what had been outward-looking maritime trading regions into peripheral parts of large landward states. So Brittany, central in the Atlantic economy, was peripheral in France. Southern Italy, an agricultural and Mediterra-nean trading region, was incorporated into an Italian economy which linked it to an industrialising north with which it had little in common. Ireland's fledgling industries were (except in the north) challenged by more efficient producers across the water. Southern France was peripheralised, except for the port of Marseille, which looked to expanding imperial markets.

It was also large states that came to define culture and refinement during the modern period. It was their languages, first French and then English, which set the international standard and which others had to learn. Small states have maintained their languages while often speaking English as well, as in Norway or the Netherlands. The awakening of the nations in the 19th century was accompanied by an awakening of the languages. Norwegian was codified (in two versions, as it happens) and demarcated from Danish, while the Slavic languages took their modern form. Stateless languages had a harder time. Some, such as Catalan, survived into moder-nity through the diligence of scholars and activists but others were not so fortunate. Abandoned by the middle classes, they were downgraded to mere dialects spoken, it was said, by 'poets and peasants'.

It is well known that historians can shape the present by writing the past. Large and small states alike have their intellectuals to write their history in a teleological manner, starting from the present and working backwards. So history, from being a haphazard series of events, becomes an inexorable process leading to the nation. So Italians and Germans can talk about 19th-century 'unification' of their countries rather than the creation, as though the nation was always there, awaiting only its full realisation. French intellectuals use the image of the 'hexagon' a geographical space with 'natural' boundaries for the French nation to fill. As the writing of history was moulded by nation states, the grand historical narratives favoured the big states at the expense of the small.

National histories also present the origins of the nation in the far mists of time, and imagine a pre-modern period of innocence. There is both truth and invention in these narratives – as Ernest Renan famously put it, nations need both to remember and to forget their pasts. It is true that the states of England, France and Spain can be traced back to the mediaeval or Renaissance epochs. Yet the nation-state, as we understand it, is much more recent, a 19th-century invention. It gained its full panoply of functions only in the mid-20th century. The nation has changed its form and the direction of its evolution many times in the past and there is no reason why in the future the size and shape of polities should not change again.

Indeed, even in the heyday of the large state, smaller units survived. Scandinavia could have become a single, albeit differentiated, state like the United Kingdom but history worked otherwise. After a series of unions and disunions, it settled down into a number of states, which jealously guard their independence and identity. The Netherlands, which was born from a religious revolt in a group of varied provinces in the 16th century, developed into a strong and unitary state. Belgium split away in 1830, only itself to experience territorial tensions in the late 20th century. Finland emerged from successive Swedish and Russian overlordship while the Baltic states emerged twice during the 20th century. In the 21st century, global change has dissolved the old certainties about the direction of history and many of these perennial questions about the size of polities and the importance of boundaries.

Global Imperatives

During the 1990s, the debate about 'globalisation' again posed the question of the size of states and their adaptation to world conditions. Globalisation, which was never clearly defined, referred to the integration of economies, cultures and, in some versions, politics on a world scale. International trade flows, it was argued, made the idea of national economies meaningless.

Free movement of capital could overwhelm efforts by governments to manage their currencies, as speculative circulation of money dwarfed the sums needed to sustain trade. Transnational corporations could shift investment and production at will, so forcing national governments to meet their wishes in matters of taxation and regulation. It is a moot point whether such corporations are truly stateless or are actually rooted in the USA and perhaps a few other big states, but either way small states appeared to be marginalised. There is a cultural version of the globalisation, which refers to the rise of global culture based on mass consumerism – again whether this is truly global or really American did not alter the equation much. The information revolution was another contributing factor, with trade in goods giving way to information and instant communications breaking down national borders.

The outcome of all this was a booming literature on the 'end of the nation-state' or, in some versions, the 'end of territory', which was taken to mean much the same thing. Indeed one book, published in English as *The End of the Nation-State* (Guéhenno, 2000), had appeared earlier in French with the apocalyptic title of *La fin de la démocratie* (The end of democracy) (Guéhenno, 1993), such is the French association of the nation-state with modernisation and progress. At the same time, in the euphoria of the end of the Cold War, some American scholars pronounced the 'end of history' (Fukuyama, 1992), which had culminated in the triumph of American liberal capitalism. Marxist historian Eric Hobsbawm (1990), for his part, announced the end of nations and nationalism, which had their birth in the late 18th century and met their demise in the late 20th. Nationalisms of the modern period were merely Hegel's Owl of Minerva, which flies by night. In other words, they were the dying flight of an older order.

In retrospect, all this talk of globalisation and the end of nations and states proved overblown. Critics talked of 'globalony', arguing that it was a cover for the imposition of neo-liberal economic discipline on the entire world or for US domination. Certainly nations and nationalism have not disappeared. On the contrary, they have thrived, often precisely in opposition to the various elements of the globalisation paradigm. Nor have states faded away; they have instead proliferated. Currently the United Nations has 193 members, against 154 in 1980. It is true, however, that the freedom of action of nation-states has been highly circumscribed by economic forces over which they have ever less control. States with their own currencies are vulnerable to speculative attacks, as the United Kingdom experienced in 1992. States with high taxes on companies and wealthy individuals may risk losing investment and tax base as these take their incomes and assets elsewhere. As capital and production could so easily be moved around it became ever more difficult to tax corporations at all. The result was a gradual reduction in corporate taxation and a blind eye to tax avoidance by big firms. Recent revelations about the taxes paid (or not paid) by the likes of Starbucks, Amazon and Microsoft illustrate the point. International regimes such as the World Trade Organisation and the European Union have strict competition rules to promote a level playing field. These restrict the ability of states to protect their own producers and to intervene in the economy in a whole range of ways. Of course, it is in principle open to states to opt out of these regimes, but the economic cost of doing so is so large (except perhaps for some resource-rich countries) as to be prohibitive.

Financial markets have gone global, so that governments seeking borrowing and credit must obey their disciplines. During the 2000s, a major constraint on governments has been their credit ratings, which govern their access to capital markets and ability to borrow. These markets are often presented as disembodied forces responding to objective forces, but they in fact consist of people with a particular view of the world making judgements that are by no means always rational. Private credit-rating agencies, by awarding or taking away points, can determine whether governments can borrow and at what rates. A negative rating can have devastating consequences.

Many people have argued that, in the age of globalisation, the Keynesian macroeconomic management of the post-war years is no longer possible. If a government seek to stimulate the national economy by spending, the effects of stimulus will leak away into other countries as people spend their money on imports. Persistent deficits will push up borrowing costs. Perhaps the most-cited example of this is France in the early 1980s, when the socialist President Mitterrand started in office with a Keynesian reflation, only to be forced into a U-turn within two years. Mitterrand, it is said, had to face hard reality. The truth is, as so often, rather different from the spin that was put on it. Mitterrand's stimulus package was in fact rather modest. The French balance of payments remained in better shape than that of the UK under the contemporary Thatcher government while both the budget and balance of payments deficits were lower than those being racked up by Ronald Reagan in the United States. This suggests that there is a large element of interpretation in all of this. Governments with apparently sound finance credentials can get away with more irresponsible spending policies than can social democrats, since they have the confidence of the markets. Again, this suggests that globalisation is something that is not entirely objective and at least to a degree is politically constructed.

One response to globalisation has been emergence of the 'competition state', an idea with its modern origins in the work of Michael Porter (1990). Classical economic trade theory worked on the principle of comparative advantage elaborated by David Ricardo in the 19th century. This holds that output and efficiency are maximised when each country specialises in that activity at which it is best. It does not have to be better than other countries at any particular activity. So, to use Ricardo's example, Portugal might be cheaper than England in producing both wine and wheat but should specialise in wine (where it has the comparative advantage) while England should do the wheat. In conditions of free trade, production would naturally sort out according to comparative advantage. In recent years, however, there has been an emphasis on competitive, or absolute, advantage. The claim is that, particularly in high technology production, there is an absolute level of performance, which gives permanent advantages to some producers. There is only so much space within global niches so that nations are in competition to occupy them. As Porter (1990: 8) puts it: 'exposure to international competition creates for each industry an absolute productivity standard necessary to meet foreign rivals, not a relative productivity standard compared to other industries within its national economy'. Hence his title *The Competitive Advantage of Nations*.

It should be said that Porter's arguments are not always clear. He asks 'Why do some nations succeed and others fail in international competition?' (Porter, 1990: 1), but later he argues 'We must abandon the whole notion of a "competitive nation" as a term having much meaning for economic prosperity' (Porter, 1990: 66). What he seems to be saying is that states (nations are another matter) should create the conditions for firms to prosper, but he returns consistently to the idea that they are competing. Management consultants then make a very good living out of telling each country how it can become more competitive, echoing the advice of the Red Queen in *Alice in Wonderland*: 'Now, here, you see, it takes all the running you can do, to keep in the same place. If you want to get somewhere else, you must run at least twice as fast as that!'

At its crudest, this becomes a kind of neo-mercantilism reminiscent of the early modern era, when it was believed that countries could only prosper at the expense of each other. Simplistic formulations such as 'UK plc.' suggest that everyone in the country has the same interest and that the nation is some kind of profit-maximising corporation. This implies that everything in the country should be subordinated to this idea of economic competition. A further move (building on Porter) is to assume that there is only one way to compete effectively and that this is to adopt the business-driven view of the world and the neo-liberal prospectus. So all virtue lies in the private market and the public sector is a drain on resources. A competitive national economy, on this reasoning, can only be a deregulated one with low taxes, in which capital is free to act as it pleases.

While it is true that the global economy is restructuring and rescaling and that states face new constraints on their policy capacity, the deterministic arguments about the imperatives of the global competitive economy have been overplayed and heavily influenced by the ideological preferences of their proponents. They have provided a pretext for neo-liberal doctrines in the guise of objective necessity; as Margaret Thatcher put it, there is no alternative (TINA). They also supply a rationale for reducing the influence of labour in favour of capital, on the grounds that capital is mobile while labour is not and that trade unions are a drag on competitiveness.

Social democrats and others on the left argue that this emphasis on competition and accommodating capital will lead to a 'race to the bottom', as states cut regulation and taxes, and thus social spending. In a competitive world, no amount of cuts can give a country a permanent advantage, so the race to cut will continue indefinitely. This may fatally undermine national welfare states.

National welfare states can also be undermined by the unbalancing of social relationships under globalisation. Welfare states were built on social compromises between capital and labour in a situation in which neither had an 'exit' option so that they were obliged to accommodate each other. If capital and highly skilled workers can now move around while the rest of the labour force is immobile, there is less incentive to come to these agreements. Multinational firms, in particular, are often known for their anti-trade union attitudes and unwillingness to engage in broader bargaining. So the decline of trade unions has been linked to the internationalisation of the economy and a division between workers in more or less globalised sectors. This in turn has unbalanced domestic political compromises between capital and labour that underpinned the post-war welfare state. This may pose an existential threat to national welfare states. Again, the argument may have been exaggerated. European welfare states have, in spite of retrenchment, survived. Margaret Thatcher's ambition to roll back the state was never realised, although another Conservative-led government returned to this goal after 2010. Welfare states have not only survived under pressure but they continue to take very different forms across European states, rooted in historical patterns and policy choices.

All this presents huge challenges for the state in its role in managing the economy and sustaining social welfare. It explains a lot of the increase in social inequality across many western societies in recent decades. On the other hand, it is a mistake to see states merely as the passive victim of impersonal global forces. Indeed states may themselves have been among the promoters of globalisation in pursuit of their own objectives. Politics still matter and institutions matter. States do have instruments for managing their own economies at their command, but they may be different from those used in the past. For example, given the ineffectiveness of Keynesian macroeconomic tools, the focus of policy might shift to supply-side measures aimed at boosting productivity. Nor is it the case that competitiveness requires that states engage in neo-liberal deregulation and tax cutting. As we will discuss in the next chapter, neo-liberalism may be bad for its own health. There are indeed other modes of managing the economy and reaching national compromises on social and economic questions.

CHAPTER 3

Small is Beautiful?

The Return of Small States

IF ALL STATES were impotent in the face of globalisation and competitive imperatives then *a fortiori* small states should be even more disempowered. They are even less able to master global forces, to balance their economies or to resist external pressure. Lacking large internal markets, they must export and accept the disciplines of the global economy. Yet from the 1980s some observers noted that small European states were not only surviving but often doing rather well. In defiance of the 'race to the bottom' these tended to have rather large public sectors and high taxes. Rodrik (1998) attributed this to the needs of economic stabilisation. While large states could mobilise resources over a larger space and recover from downturns more easily, small states were more vulnerable to economic fluctuations, which a larger public sector could help to cushion. Small states tended to be open economically, seeking global markets to compensate for their small domestic ones, and supporting trade liberalisation (Katzenstein, 1985). Many of them focused on specialised types of production in which economies of scale are less important than in the basic industries of the old industrial era. Global and European free trade regimes reduce the capacity of states to manage their economies in the old way but for small states they can be liberating. They no longer need large domestic markets, since the home market is now the whole of Europe or even the world. International rules protect them by outlawing protectionism and trade barriers and preventing large states bullying them or unilaterally changing the rules. There is no longer a danger of a retreat to the protectionism that destroyed the international trading system in the interwar years. In this context, small states may gain more real autonomy than they have lost.

The same argument can be made about defence and national security. Collectivisation of security under NATO and other transnational bodies reduces threats from neighbours as well as more remote powers. It eliminates the need for autonomous national defence or costly armaments across the whole spectrum. Small states have adapted to this in various ways. Some, such as Denmark and Norway, joined NATO, while Austria was neutral by international agreement. Finland was neutral but with a care not to provoke the Soviet Union, while Sweden practised armed neutrality. Ireland was formally neutral, for historic reasons, but not politically impartial between east and west and was able effectively to free ride on western security since the western powers would not allow it to fall into the hands of their enemies. All these countries effectively sheltered under the umbrella of NATO, which prevented wars within the western sphere.

To those with a historical sensitivity, this is not so surprising. As we have seen, there have been different types of polity throughout history, with conditions variously favouring the large and the small. If the first half of the 20th century suggested that a state needed to be big to look after itself, the second half showed that there were other ways. The end of the Cold War meant the end of the external threat that had helped to pull western Europe together and pool its defence, but collective security arrangements have survived. At the same time, the collapse of the Soviet Union and Yugoslavia produced yet more small states, including the Baltic countries (Latvia, Lithuania and Estonia), the Czech and Slovak republics, Slovenia, Croatia, Bosnia and Herzegovina, Serbia, Montenegro and (a still disputed case) Kosovo. While these countries harbour strong nationalist movements committed to the restoration of sovereignty, they are well aware of the limitations of statehood and their governments have consistently sought shelter in European economic and security structures.

Global and European changes have not only provided a new external support system for small states. They have also encouraged claims from nationalist movements within large states. There is a passive side of this, as the old states lose their capacity to master their territories, and an active side, as sub-state national movements fashion their own alternatives. Large states have, in many cases, lost their old hegemony in determining identities and moulding their populations. Broadcasting ceased to be a state monopoly by the 1980s. Migration has introduced multiple cultures. Technological developments are constantly freeing communications from state control, however much the latter may seek to re-impose discipline.

Internationalisation of the economy, together with global and European trading and competition rules, have eliminated many of the old regional policy mechanisms that states used to tie their territories together.

The social and political bargain underpinning regional policy has weakened. Citizens in wealthy regions can no longer be sure that money transferred to their poorer compatriots will return in the form of orders for their products. Firms, being international and mobile, can no longer be arm-twisted into investing in poor regions of the homeland when they can go to cheaper locations abroad. The emphasis on national competitiveness means that states may prefer to build on their stronger regions rather than help the poorest to catch up. So just as states have adopted the language of international competition in global markets, so the theme of competitiveness has replaced that of cohesion between cities and regions within states. The European Commission has joined in the game, enjoining regions to be become more competitive.

Nationalist movements, especially in wealthy places, have latched on to this as a reason for becoming independent, or at least gaining maximum autonomy. While in the past, nationalism was often associated with poorer regions with an economic grievance, a revolt of the poor, now some people write of a revolt of the rich as regions and stateless nations seek to join the body of small states rather than remaining within the larger ones that no longer seem to be working in their interests.

Support for smaller units also comes from a body of theory in economic geography known as the 'new regionalism'. This draws on an old idea, that territory might be a vital factor in economic development. The notion goes back to the 19th century when Alfred Marshall noted that particular industries tended to cluster together in industrial districts, where they could sustain each other and concentrate supply chains and knowledge. He even suggested that there might a cultural element, 'something in the air' beyond mere economic interdependence. These ideas fell out of favour during the 20th century as economists insisted that places were very much alike, apart from the factor of distance and the presence or absence of raw materials. As communications improved and the advanced economic sectors became less dependent on primary production, even these became less important; this was one part of the globalisation thesis. From the 1990s, however, economic geographers have rediscovered industrial districts and, more broadly, the importance of space. In this conception, space is more than just proximity to markets and raw materials and connection among supply chains. It is vital to cooperation and communication among producers, especially in innovative sectors. The old 'traded interdependencies' of suppliers and manufacturers are complemented by 'untraded interdependencies' in the form of shared knowledge, skills and innovation. These are fostered in particular locales, often through informal contacts and day-to-day transactions. Some observers go further and attribute the success of particular places to cultural norms and practices, learned over time. There has been a debate over 'social capital', an ill-defined term but which refers to the capacity of communities to innovate and cooperate in the pursuit of common interests (we discuss this later). The new economy privileges skills, knowledge and entrepreneurship, which may also be fostered within local communities.

In this way, territories are not merely locations of production but production systems in their own right, with an internal logic that is self-reinforcing. A further stage in the argument is to see these systems as being in competition, just as nations are seen as competing. The idea has been embraced by states, which, unable to manage their spatial economies as in the past, have downloaded the responsibility to regions, telling them to become more competitive. The European Commission has spread the same idea, with a relentless message about regional competitiveness. Of course, since competitiveness is always measured in relation to one's competitors, it is impossible for all regions to become more competitive at the same time, as opposed to becoming more productive. The theme, however, is in tune with the ideological tone of the times. It has been taken up by nationalist movements in wealthy regions, who argue, as we have seen, that they should not be held back by their weaker compatriots.

Such competition could reinforce the 'race to the bottom', with regions and stateless nations striving to escape the embrace of their host states but still trapped by the dictates of global competitiveness. One of the most insistent arguments against independence for stateless nations (and notably for Scotland) is that it will undermine the welfare state, which is based on state-wide solidarity and the ability of a large state to shift resources on a wide scale and to address asymmetrical shocks. Yet it does not appear to be the case that large states are better at welfare and distribution than smaller ones. On the contrary, the most generous welfare provision and the highest levels of public services are found in some of the smaller states. It may be that the size of the state is less important than the degree of solidarity found within it. We know that the European Union has a very large territory and population but has not generated a strong degree of solidarity. The Nordic countries, on the other hand, have small populations and high solidarity. Indeed it may be that social solidarity operates at multiple levels, from the neighbourhood to the world, in different ways and that the best place to realise it depends on the circumstances.

Small states' macroeconomic options are highly restricted. They are, in many ways, policy takers rather than policy makers (Skilling, 2012). So they must adapt. The key to adaptation is flexibility, embodied in policies, institutions and social practices. Small states may have some advantages here in that their leaders, whether in government, business and civil society, know each other personally and there are short lines of communication. The relevant people can gather in one room to sort out deals. There may be less social distance between groups and a sense of shared destiny. The challenges of facing a dangerous world may foster a habit of working together and a sense of social cohesion. The power of large vested interests may be less.

On the other hand, we could suggest a contrary hypothesis. Small states, where everyone knows everyone else, could be risk-averse and prone to group-think. The need for consensus could stifle innovation and creativity. Vested interests could be stronger and domestic producers could be in a strong position to demand protection and support of various sorts, to inhibit economic change and dynamism. The very closeness of actors may encourage rent-seeking, in which groups each try to enlarge their own share of the pie rather than expanding the pie itself. Interest groups representing outdated and uncompetitive sectors may exercise undue influence.

There is also a danger of clientelism, a mode of government based on doing favours for individuals and small groups and distributing resources in small packages. This avoids large issues and prevents resources being applied where they can produce the largest social benefit. It also discourages long-term planning. Some scholars have seen clientelism as a remnant of the 'patrimonial' relations of traditional society, based on individual links and exchange, which will die out with modernisation. Others see it as the product of a transition to modernity, as individuals need to find a way to cope with big impersonal structures. Others again argue that it can perpetuate itself even in modern societies, shaping the form that modernity itself takes. Since clientelism depends on delivering small and visible favours, a job here, a road there, a grant in another place, and on individual politicians getting the credit, it may thrive in small societies where people know each other and reputations are important. In larger states, these matters may be dealt with by an impersonal bureaucracy, while the population is so large that politicians are unable to bribe them all.

It all depends on how small states are organised. Before exploring the different modes of adaption, must pause to address some of the more simplistic formulations that have become popular in recent times.

Reductionisms

Just as there were prophets of the inevitability of large states in the 20th century, so in recent years there have been seers who predict the opposite. Some prominent commentators have argued that, because big states are no longer needed in a globalised world and small states may be more efficient, the old nation-state is doomed to break up into more manageable units. Kenichi Ohmae's (1995) *The End of the Nation State: The Rise of Regional Economies*, in its very title equates the rise of the region with the end of the state. The assumption here is that the nation is a mere economic machine, which must and does adapt to global economic imperatives. From Ohmae's neo-liberal perspective, the only mode of adaptation is to accept market discipline, cut back on the welfare state and privilege business interests. He then cites some rather unlikely examples of successful adaptation. As so often with popular books, the weakness of the argument is offset by its simplicity and the work has been widely cited.

Another much-mentioned work is Alesina and Spoloare's (2003) *The Size of Nations*. They too equate the nation with the state and reduce both to an economic machine. They argue that since, in the era of free trade, the big state is not needed to secure markets, it will disappear. This, they think, is both inevitable and desirable, which is why the argument has appealed to certain nationalists. They even argue that, historically, new states have been formed in times of free trade. This is simply untrue. In fact, most small states are the result of decolonisation or, in Europe, the fall of empires, including the Habsburg, Ottoman and Russian empires after the First World War and the Soviet Union in the late 20th century and had nothing whatever to do with free trade. The aftermath of the First World War led to protectionism and some of the new states, like Ireland, consciously adopted protectionist policies during the 1930s. Economic considerations hardly featured in early 20th-century debates about independence, which were driven by nation-building and identity politics, and nationalists tended to be economic protectionists (Bohle and Greskovits, 2013). Like Ohmae, Alesina and Spoloare fall into functional reductionism in arguing that because something may have economic consequences, that is why it happened. This ignores the critical role of politics and political choice.

Another of Alesina and Spoloare's arguments is that smaller states will better serve their citizens by giving them policies that they like. This is a superficially appealing argument but, in this version, is actually quite incoherent and leads to some alarming conclusions. They start from public goods theory. It is assumed that people know what policies they prefer and that the task of government is to realise these preferences. Small states are more desirable because, with a smaller population, their citizens are more likely to have the same preferences for public policies. In fact, this does not follow since there is no particular reason to think that a population of five million people is more likely to agree among themselves than one of fifty million. Some of the smallest states and regions are deeply divided.

Alesina and Spoloare, however, prop up their argument about people in small places sharing preferences by assuming that small regions and countries will be more ethnically homogeneous. So the argument is not just about small states but about small, ethnic states. As they put it, 'in today's world of free trade, relatively small ethnic regions can "afford" to stay small and homogeneous' (p. 14). Now this is entering a minefield. Ethnicity is a highly problematic concept. Sociologists these days are practically unanimous in thinking that it is not something inherent in individuals but is socially constructed – it is the product, not the cause, of mobilisation. Individuals have multiple identities, which they use for different purposes – class, gender, nationality or age for example – and share these differently with different other people. In so far as ethnicity can be measured, it is inevitably seen as a compound of other characteristics including language, religion, subjective feelings and intersubjective meanings, which are always contested and always changing. Race, a term that Alesina and Spoloare also use rather freely, is even more problematic. Biologists are agreed that it is not a scientific category. It is rather a sociological category, in which an arbitrary characteristic like skin colour is used to unite people who are otherwise highly varied and to differentiate them from others.

The concepts of ethnicity and race are questionable not only on sociological grounds, but also on normative or ethical ones. They are deeply loaded terms and subject to a great deal of argument. It is widely accepted in liberal political thought that race should not be the basis for forming polities or determining preferences. Yet Alesina and Spoloare seem to think that white, African American and Hispanic people in the United States will have different preferences in education, despite the fact that a generation of civil rights activists fought to integrate education systems. In the famous *Brown vs. Board of Education* decision, the US Supreme Court ruled that even 'separate but equal' education systems were unconstitutional.

It is also widely accepted within liberal political thought that ethnicity provides a poor basis for founding states. As it is defined so arbitrarily and is so difficult to measure, there can never be agreement on the boundaries of groups and, even to the extent that it can, they are never neatly concentrated in one place so allowing us to draw territorial boundaries around them. Making ethnicity the basis for statehood just encourages losing groups within the new state to create or reaffirm their own ethnic credentials, so producing an infinite regress. The result can be a succession of secessions, hence the term Balkanisation.

Moreover, 'ethnic nationalism', which requires strict adherence to ascriptive criteria (that is, things that individuals cannot change) is nowadays seen as morally dubious. This, as we have noted, is where Alesina and Spoloare went wrong. It is a violation of equal citizenship and liberal principles. Homogeneity has been achieved only (after the two world wars) by compulsory transfers of population or, more brutally, ethnic cleansing. Even in Bosnia and Herzegovina, where the international community reluctantly accepted the existence of ethnically-based entities, it has insisted that these should not officially be based on ethnicity and that minorities within them should have equal rights.

The Civic Nation

It is for this reason that nationalists in Scotland and liberal nationalists elsewhere have insisted that theirs is a civic project for the realisation of an inclusive nation. This is built, not on ethnic homogeneity, but on a shared political identity. This opens up an argument for the nation based on entirely different premises. It is not a place for conformity and consensus but a deliberative space in which political differences can be debated and resolved through majorities or through compromise. A nation does not have a single, economically determined interest but contains the whole spectrum of social classes and economic sectors. It is a place where opposition thrives and where political minorities can become majorities.

Some of the literature on nationalism assumes that the nationalism of the large states is a civic one but that of the stateless nations must necessarily be ethnic, an argument we met at the beginning of this chapter. This appears to be the thrust of Joseph Weiler's (2013) argument, even if he does not use those exact terms. It is the employed by Ralph Dahrendorf (1995), a German Liberal (who became a member of the British House of Lords). The ethnic exclusiveness or civic inclusiveness of a particular nationalist movement, in fact, has nothing to do with whether it the nation happens to have its own state. Indeed, at the time Dahrendorf wrote the paper we have quoted, Germany had an ethnically exclusive citizenship law, while Catalonia was making great efforts to integrate incomers into the national community. Weiler did not even bother to explore the basis for Spanish nationalism (which actually has both a civic-republican and a reactionary-religious-exclusive traditions) while condemning the Catalan version.

This does not mean, as is sometimes assumed, that a civic nationalism is not a nationalism at all. All nationalisms seek to define the boundaries of the political community in a particular way. So the British nationalist (we might say UK nationalist if there was such an adjective) would define the political community in one way and the Scottish nationalist in another, but both could insist that theirs is a civic project, which includes everybody within the boundary whatever their origins. A similar argument can be made about Spain and Catalonia, while Basque nationalism in recent decades has moved beyond the exclusive ethnic particularism of its founder, Sabino Arana. Drawing the boundaries may indeed have consequences for public policies, not because people on either side are essentially different but because the outcomes of political deliberation and social compromise may diverge both in the short term and over longer periods as institutions take on their own dynamics. Shared identities may develop not on the basis of ethnic exclusiveness but because of shared historical experiences. These are never hegemonic and co-exist with other identities and interests that shape policy preferences. They may underpin the legitimacy of institutions so that losers will accept the outcome, but on condition that losers have the opportunity to become winners in a future round.

Nations thus constructed may be states, federal units or devolved jurisdictions. In any of these cases, they are enmeshed in complex relationships of interdependency, with neighbours, partners and the market.

Small nations are particularly caught up in this web of interdependencies, working within parameters that are set elsewhere. This does not mean that they are powerless but their adaptation to external change and to the global order requires specific skills and ways of working that are not the same as those of big states, for whom sovereignty is backed by economic and military force. In the next chapter, we explore the strategies available for small states to chart their economic and social futures and the terms of their engagement with the global economy.

CHAPTER 4

The High Road and the Low Road

The Competition State

THERE IS, AS WE have seen, some truth in the idea that states compete against each other, but only some. The idea of competition has become so dominant in modern times that it has spread well beyond the world of economic markets and sport into all domains of public life, so that universities, the arts, schools and (in England) even hospitals compete. Even in areas where proper markets do not operate, like education (where the consumer by definition does not know exactly what should be supplied), artificial or quasi-markets are constructed. The effect is often to subordinate other areas of social life to the utilitarian dictates of the economy in the narrow sense and, within the economy itself, to privilege a particular view of how it should work. Social scientists have recently been trying to get away from Gross Domestic Product as the only measure of wellbeing and have experimented with human development and even 'happiness' indices (Helliwell, Layard and Sachs, 2013), as we discuss later in the chapter. That said, we do live in a world constrained by market forces. Most democratic governments aim to deliver economic growth, and Europeans are accustomed to rising incomes and public services. Small states are particularly dependent on the global market, their domestic markets being so small and, not surprisingly, they are preoccupied with competitiveness.

One factor in international competitiveness is the currency and the exchange rate. Countries with their own currency can devalue in order to regain competitiveness by reducing export prices and increasing prices of imports. Yet having one's own currency can be a source of vulnerability as it is open to speculative movements of capital and even to deliberate undermining. British politicians are still traumatised by the notorious events of Black Wednesday in 1992 when the UK was forced out of the European Exchange Rate Mechanism. Speculators operate by selling currency to drive its exchange rate down, and then buying it back at the lower rate. Small countries may be particularly vulnerable, since their reserves are so small. The alternative is to abandon one's own currency and to join a currency union. This may be the Euro, which is managed by the European Central Bank, which has day-to-day independence but is responsible to EU member states. The Scottish Government has proposed a similar form of currency union, but between an independent Scotland and the rest of the United Kingdom. Alternatively, a small state may adopt the currency of another state, or 'peg' its currency to it so maintaining a constant parity. Either way, sharing a currency imposes a strict discipline in that devaluation is impossible and that monetary policy, including control of interest rates, passes into the hands of the European Central Bank or the monetary authority of the other state. Adjustment to changes in external economic conditions, including lost competitiveness must be managed by internal change, getting costs back in line through what is sometimes known as 'internal devaluation', including wage restraint. Adopting or pegging to a foreign currency has the further constraint that the state has no say at all over monetary policy.

All EU states with the exception of Denmark and the United Kingdom (which have opt-outs) are expected in due course to adopt the European common currency, the Euro. Denmark reaffirmed its opt-out in a referendum in 2000. Yet, while not joining the Euro, Denmark has pegged its currency to it, so accepting the associated disciplines. Sweden does not have an opt-out but has also voted by referendum not to join and allows its currency to float. Estonia operated a currency peg to the German Mark and then the Euro, in order to ensure strict monetary discipline, before entering into the Euro. Other small European states, like the Czech Republic, while officially obliged to join the Euro, show no intention of doing so any time soon.

States within the Eurozone are obliged to accept strict limits on their budget deficits as well as on accumulated debt. As some states got into trouble, these rules were tightened by successive measures passed during the 2000s so that, in effect, the European Commission is able to inspect their government accounts and intervene if they look like breaking the rules. Countries outside the Eurozone are not subject to these requirements but are in many ways subject to the same disciplines in order to maintain confidence in their currencies, especially when these are pegged to the Euro. The latter are arguably in the worst position of all, since they have to accept monetary policies, including interest rates, set in the Eurozone but have no say in the rules under which these are set.

This all imposes tight constraints on the freedom of action of small states, with or without their own currencies, especially in their ability to run up deficits and debts and to counter economic cycles through Keynesian stimulus policies. Yet these constraints do not completely curtail the scope for independent policy. Monetary discipline limits debts and deficits but, as long as they balance their books, small states are free to have either high or low levels of public expenditure. Indeed the evidence is that, even before currency union, small states practised rather prudent fiscal policies (Katzenstein, 1985). They tended not to run up large deficits, since this exposed them to external creditors and currency risks.

Within these constraints, there are, contrary to Ohmae and the neo-liberal school, multiple ways of adapting; indeed there are probably as many modes of adaptation as there are countries. To understand the logic of adaptations, however, we will examine two contrasting models. These are what Max Weber called ideal-types, simplified versions of the world, which enable us to understand key features of reality. These are the 'market liberal' mode associated with the free-market (or 'neo-liberal') right, and the alternative 'social investment' mode. Each mode has its own logic and it is not easy simply to mix and match elements of different modes.

The Liberal Market Model

The market liberal mode of adaptation accepts the logic of global competition and seeks to go with the flow. If we are competing in world markets, production costs must be kept low. If investment capital is mobile then investors must be given incentives to come. If skilled workers and professionals can move, then they must be induced to stay. Firms must be allowed to do whatever they need to be competitive and not be hampered by regulations or costs. Wages must be flexible downwards as well as upwards so as to adjust to market conditions and ensure that workers do not price themselves out of employment in difficult times. The policy recipe that flows from these assumptions includes low taxes on business and light regulation. Market liberals see the public sector as a charge on the productive economy and so try to keep it small. Labour markets are deregulated and trade unions discouraged in order to allow wage flexibility, easy hiring and firing, and the redeployment of workers. Rates of personal income tax on higher earners are low and wage differentials are high, providing high salaries for managers in order to incentivise them. Market liberals have often advocated flat rate taxes in place of progressive taxes by which higher earners pay a higher rate.

Ideally, there should be free movement of labour so that in bad times workers can migrate while in good times they come back. The market liberal strategy of going with the economic flow entails accepting economic cycles and the 'creative destruction' they can bring. In bad times, incomes and employment will fall sharply, on the argument that they can then recover faster.

New Zealand embarked on a market liberal experiment in the 1980s after it had lost a large part of its export market when the United Kingdom joined the (then) European Economic Community and its protectionist industrial strategy became unaffordable. It went on to become the 'poster child' of reform. Thatcherism in the United Kingdom had the same ambitions, although, as a larger and more complex state, with entrenched programmes and interests, it did not go as far.

The market liberal strategy has been applied widely in the Baltic States, where it can be presented as a logical part of the transition to the market economy. Trade unions are generally weak, and workers and the general public more tolerant of sharp changes in their material conditions, given their recent experiences (Bohle and Greskovits, 2013). Enlargement of the European Union has provided opportunities for out-migration when jobs are scarce and to return when times are better. Since joining the EU, all the Baltic states have had a steady outflow of workers – in 2012 this was between 4 and 25 per 1,000 of the population (Eurostat figures).

However they might work in transition countries, it is difficult to reproduce these conditions elsewhere. In a mature welfare state, public services cannot easily be dismantled. Trade unions have been greatly weakened in western Europe, but they are still part of the national life. Voters will not gladly tolerate sharp fluctuations in living standards – we have seen how austerity policies have provoked social and political instability in southern Europe. It is true that taxes on businesses in Europe have tended to be driven down by international competition, with new EU member states having some of the lowest levels. There does not, however, appear to be evidence that small countries as such have been forced to bring down their rates (Elschner and Vanborren, 2009).

More widely, it is not at all clear that the market liberal strategy will work even on its own terms. Studies have questioned the effectiveness of low corporation taxes in attracting industrial investment (Krugman, 2003;

Nathan, 2012). In mature industrial economies, they are likely to benefit existing business more than new inward investors – European rules prevent them being given only to the latter. The case of Ireland is perhaps an exception since it cut corporation tax at a time when there was little domestic industry and little existing revenue to lose. A similar argument might be made about the eastern European cases. Marginal differences in taxation also appear to be rather low down the list of criteria for choosing investment locations, compared with skilled labour, infrastructure and other locational characteristics. Tax cutting also encourages 'brass-plate' relocations in which a firm officially moves its headquarters to the low-tax country while keeping its production at home. Another dodge is transfer pricing, whereby profits are declared in the low-tax jurisdiction but production is done somewhere else, where wages are lower. If one small jurisdiction cuts taxes to bid investment away from its neighbours, this will likely trigger off a round of tax competition in which everyone cuts taxes and all lose out on revenue while ending up in the same competitive position. So one could argue that small states have an interest in harmonising corporate taxation since in any 'race to the bottom' they will be likely to end up as the losers, not being able to offer the same incentives as big countries.

The logical consequence of the low-tax regime is lower revenue for public services. Some people have argued that tax cuts can actually pay for themselves by boosting demand or giving incentives to work harder. One version of this is the so-called Laffer curve, named after an American economist but actually drawing on earlier ideas suggesting that at a certain point raising taxes does not increase revenue since it kills off economic activity. This was taken up in the political world and simplified to the notion that cutting tax rates will actually increase revenues by stimulating more economic activity. There is a large element of wishful thinking in this. Campaigning against Ronald Reagan for the Republican presidential nomination in 1980, George Bush Sr. called it 'voodoo economics', and indeed the outcome was ballooning deficits. Cutting taxes may stimulate the economy by increasing demand at a time of recession but, in normal times, if there is no spare capacity, this will not work. The other argument, that it will incentivise people to work harder, depends on the old idea that, in order to make rich people work harder you need to pay them more but to make poor people work hard we should pay them less.

Nor are low wages the best way to compete in a globalised economy, since there will always be competitors able to bring their labour costs below those of European states. Instead, successful European countries tend to foster high-wage, high-productivity activities in which their technological lead and skills can be used to best advantage.

The market liberal model is marked by sharp inequalities in income and wealth. This is because mobile firms, managers and professionals can command higher incomes – because of the weakness of trade unions – and because high incomes are used as work incentives. This may be considered socially and politically undesirable, according to one's political preferences. There is also evidence that inequality, far from stimulating economic growth, may be a drag on performance (Stiglitz, 2012; Wilkinson and Pickett, 2010; Ostry, Berg and Charalambos, 2014).

A market liberal strategy may even be self-defeating on its own criteria to the extent that public services contribute to the conditions for a productive and competitive economy. Small states may be even more in need of these public goods, as they lack the large private corporations, which might invest heavily in research and development. As a consequence, publicly funded and university research is vital.

There are also dangers in relying on foreign direct investment, which risks creating a dependent economy – a periphery in world markets vulnerable to external changes and lacking a diverse production base. The foreign investment sector can easily become detached from the domestic economy, trading in global markets and generating profits but without spreading the benefits into the host country. Small local firms may find difficulty in competing with multinational enterprises, able to offer higher wages for the most skilled workers and mobilising huge resources for investment. This can create a dual economy, with sharp distinctions between a foreign-owned sector effectively able to set its own rules, and a struggling domestic sector, which becomes crowded out. Until the 1980s, indeed, dependence on foreign-owned business was seen as a problem in Scotland and other places in Europe, even while it was being encouraged. For some reason, this issue then disappeared from the political agenda and inward investment of any type was encouraged, with ownership regarded as largely irrelevant.

The Social Investment State

An alternative conception is that of the social investment state (Crouch, 2013; Hemerijck, 2013). In this model, public expenditure is not seen as a drain on the productive economy but, potentially at least, as part of it. The issue is not whether expenditure is undertaken by the public or the private sector but what it is spent on. So education represents investment in human capital while health spending can enhance productivity. Research is a contribution to innovation and economic renewal. Expenditure on childcare allows mothers with young children to remain in the labour market, so expanding the workforce and retaining skills. Investment in the early years of childhood more broadly contributes to economic prosperity, improving skills while reducing the later burden of social marginalisation. This is consistent with the increasingly popular idea that 'preventive spending' now can reduce spending needs in the future by anticipating and dealing with social problems before they get out of hand. As Hemerijck (2013, p.37) put it: 'Social investment should become future-orientated, with policies aiming to prepare individuals, families, organisations, and societies to pre-empt new social risks rather than simply repair damage after adverse contingencies produce genuine losses.'

Some of this might be mere rhetoric aimed at justifying the welfare state, at a time when critics claim that is unaffordable, by simply relabeling expenditures. Taken seriously, however, the social investment strategy implies shifting priorities from traditional, passive welfare support towards active measures aimed at getting people into employment. There is now a broad consensus that the most effective way of tackling deprivation and other social problems is to get people into work, but sharp differences on how it might be achieved. While neo-liberals favour punitive approaches to unemployment, by reducing welfare benefits and imposing strict requirements, the social welfare approach privileges preparation. So active labour market policy, seeking to align training, benefits and economic development, has become central to policy debates. Among the best known examples is the Danish 'flexicurity' model, in which labour markets are deregulated and it is possible to dismiss people rather easily – therefore helping flexibility and adaptation – but unemployed people are generously compensated and there are active measures to get them back into work.

This is all consistent with modern ideas about supply-side measures as the key to economic success, given the limitations of states, and especially small states, to engage in traditional Keynesian economic management or, within currency unions like the Euro, to use monetary policy to regulate demand. It is also consistent with the move away from the classical welfare state model based on the male breadwinner heading a family, towards a more complex society in which gender and age, as much as class, structure the labour market. There are 'new social risks' which include precarious and low-paid employment and marginalisation of under-prepared workers. The old model was based on insurance against the contingencies of life, which would balance out in due course. Unemployment was seen as cyclical so that national insurance funds could accumulate in boom times and be drawn down in recessions. Old age pensions were built up in the working years and consumed after retirement at a fixed age. Whether built up in the form of investment funds or as obligations on the part of the state, they represented claims on future production, which was generally assumed to be ever-increasing. In the new way of thinking, there are multiple types of household and routes into employment. There is also a need for continually upgrading skills to meet new technologies and modes of production.

Successful states have also been able to manage economic transformation. Past policies have often focused on retaining old industries for social reasons, even if they were outdated and unproductive. The market liberal strategy is to expose them to the winds of competition, allowing whole sectors to go to the wall and losing not only the industries but the skills base which they had accumulated; this is more or less what happened in the United Kingdom in the 1980s. Small states cannot afford to prop up unproductive industries, nor to maintain expensive and uncompetitive sectors as large states often do. They do not have the large defence budgets that have allowed the USA and the UK to sustain big military contractors. They have therefore largely abandoned efforts to prop up 'national champions' or protect them from takeovers. They have, however, sought to manage the transition in a less costly fashion than occurred in the UK in the 1980s, where the oil revenues were used to keep the state afloat amid industrial collapse. Instead, they have tried to keep and develop the skills base for use in new and emerging sectors.

It is tempting to idealise the social investment model as a magic formula which enhances both economic competitiveness and social welfare, allowing us to escape with one bound from the crucial dilemma between growth and equity. Education both improves the economy and aids social mobility by giving people from poorer backgrounds the opportunity to prosper. It is for this reason that it has been heavily favoured in many countries. Health spending can also be presented as having both economic and social benefits – in the early days of the National Health Service some people believed that it would pay for itself by reducing illness and lost production. Active labour market policies help individuals out of poverty and increase the productive labour force at the same time. Reskilling and training could ease the transition into high-productivity activities and so raise wages. As we have noted, there is evidence that more equal societies might be more productive, so that again the social and economic imperatives can be reconciled.

In practice, matters are not so straightforward. Critics have claimed that the phrase 'social investment', coined by Anthony Giddens, prophet of the 'Third Way' in social democracy, is redolent of the various attempts by New Labour rhetoric to square circles. It may amount to little more than a way of trying to justify public services at a time of financial constraint and neo-liberal hegemony. It often seems to subordinate the claims of social justice and equality to those of the economy, thus accepting the premises of neo-liberalism if not its conclusions. By focusing on productive labour, the social investment approach might favour the better-off members of society or those who could most easily be brought into the workforce (Rhodes, 2013). Trying to justify social spending by reference to its contribution to growth could distort priorities. The stress on new social risks might be exaggerated, since the old social risks, principally of cyclical unemployment, have not gone away. So no amount of preparation and job training is going to get people into work if there are not enough jobs to go around. It can merely allow politicians to blame the unemployed for their own condition, as has happened in recent times in the United Kingdom.

Social investment has often been associated with social democracy, which is essentially an effort to reconcile market capitalism with social justice. In fact, it could equally well be pursued by governments of a centre-right persuasion as a way of improving productive conditions. What distinguishes the social democratic version is an emphasis on social equality, as opposed to the equality of opportunity to which New Labour aspired. It is becoming increasingly difficult to reduce inequalities simply by redistributing income through taxes and benefits, given the massive inequalities generated in the labour market and by the new international division of labour. Such measures might be no more than palliatives, able to slow down the rise in equalities, while addressing the structure of the labour market and the preparation of individuals could do much more. Yet a social democratic approach would also accept that labour market activation is complementary to, rather than a substitute for, traditional welfare support. Although it might be broadly true that more equal societies are more productive, there is not a simple causal relationship and in many instances there are still hard choices to be made between productivist and egalitarian policies.

Equality can come about through two mechanisms. The first is the operation of labour markets, which generate more or less inequality in income. The second is through overt redistribution through taxes, benefits and services. The evidence suggests that the Nordic countries start out with relatively low wage differentials and then enhance equality further through public policies. This tends to be done through universal provision of services rather than progressive taxation. It is, contrary to widespread belief, the less equal countries that resort to progressive taxation in an effort to reduce disparities (OECD, 2012). The secret, rather, appears to be generously-funded and universal services paid for by broad-based taxes.

There are, however, some important preconditions for the social investment state. The first is that some states have a better starting point than others. Even among the transition states of eastern and central Europe, emerging from Communism, some were better placed than others because of historic legacies or because they had started to adapt even before the Berlin Wall came down (Bohle and Greskovits, 2013). An independent Scotland would not start in the same place as the Nordic countries to which it often looks for inspiration. Some of their legacies go all the way back to the 19th century while others date to historic crises and social compromises in the 20th. Second, social investment is a long-term strategy whose benefits are necessarily a long time in coming. States thus need to learn to defer consumption and immediate gratification in favour of the long term and the present generation needs to think of future ones.

Third, social investment is expensive. It may, in the long run, produce a more productive economy but it still needs to be financed, in both the long and the short term. This implies higher taxes. Given the volatility of taxes on high earners and their propensity to migrate, taxes need to be broad and weigh also on the middle classes. Politically, this is likely to be sustainable only when all citizens feel that they benefit from the public services financed by taxation. A state that limits itself to taxing the rich to redistribute benefits to the poor risks a backlash from the better-off sections of society, especially when they themselves are using private provision in matters like education, health and transport. This explains the tendency in the Nordic countries to universal rather than selectively-available public services, so binding in the whole population to the social contract. Social justice is assured by providing the same level for rich and poor rather than by explicitly redistributive tax policies.

Taxes also need to be difficult to avoid. Avoidance may be easier in small states, to the degree to which businesses and individuals can move out. There has been a tendency for corporate taxes to come down due to tax competition. Strikingly, they tend to be higher in the United States than in the social democratic states of northern Europe, since businesses are less inclined to move out of the US, although they do play off individual states in order to get concessions. The more highly taxed states tend to favour high rates on consumption, through Value Added Tax and excise duties. Another form of taxation that is difficult to avoid and cannot be escaped by moving is taxes on property but few states really exploit these because of their high visibility and hence unpopularity.

The Evidence

The empirical evidence does indeed allow us to distinguish among small states and their strategies for coping with global competition. In the next chapters, we examine the experience of the Nordic countries, with their broadly social-investment, social democratic model; the Baltic states, which have followed a market liberal strategy; and Ireland, which has been something of a hybrid. Figure 4.1 shows a clear division into high tax/ high spending Nordic states and low tax/low spending Baltics. Ireland is currently in between but this is the result of the economic crisis – historically it has been nearer the low-spending end. In particular, the Nordic states have high levels of social spending.

Tax rates show the same pattern. Latvia, Lithuania and Ireland have low corporation tax rates to attract inward investment, while Estonia taxes at 21 per cent and the rate rises to 28 per cent in Norway (Figure 4.2). Despite the undoubted pressures to convergence, there are still significant differences among neighbouring countries, which would not be expected if all were engaged in a race to the bottom.

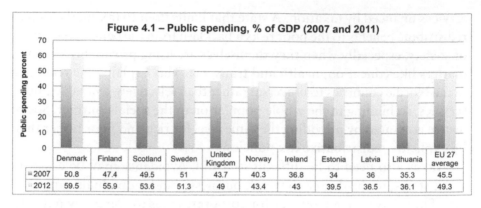

Figure 4.1 – Public spending, % of GDP (2007 and 2011)

	Denmark	Finland	Scotland	Sweden	United Kingdom	Norway	Ireland	Estonia	Latvia	Lithuania	EU 27 average
2007	50.8	47.4	49.5	51	43.7	40.3	36.8	34	36	35.3	45.5
2012	59.5	55.9	53.6	51.3	49	43.4	43	39.5	36.5	36.1	49.3

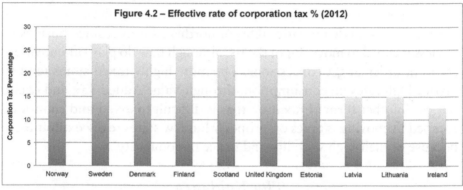

Figure 4.2 – Effective rate of corporation tax % (2012)

Marginal rates of income tax vary from a low of 15 per cent in Lithuania to a high of 56.6 per cent in Sweden (Figure 4.3). Value added taxes show less variation, and there are European limits to how much is allowed, but the social investment states tend to tax to the limit (Figure 4.4); they also have fewer VAT exemptions than the United Kingdom.

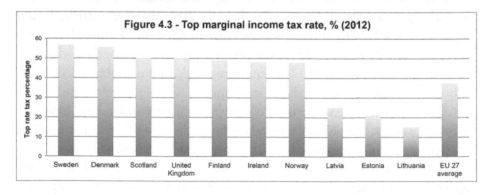

Figure 4.3 - Top marginal income tax rate, % (2012)

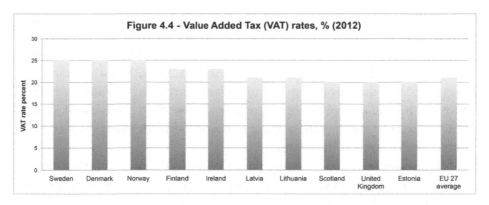

Figure 4.4 - Value Added Tax (VAT) rates, % (2012)

One effect is that economic inequalities are lower in the Nordic group, higher in the Baltics, with the United Kingdom and Ireland in between. This is measured by the Gini coefficient, shown in Table 4.1, where a higher figure means less inequality. In the conventional view, these high levels of spending and inequality should lead to a loss of competitiveness and hence of wealth.

Table 4.1 – GINI coefficient					
Country	GINI coefficient	Year	Country	GINI coefficient	Year
Finland	26.9	2000	United Kingdom	34.0	2005
Sweden	25.0	2000	Latvia	36.6	2008
Denmark	24.0	2005	Estonia	36.0	2004
Norway	25.8	2000	Lithuania	37.6	2008
Ireland	34.3	2000			
Source: World Bank (2012)					

A country's standard of living is likely to be dependent on many things, including inherited wealth and natural resources. Separating out competitiveness from the other factors is necessarily difficult since there is not always agreement on what competitiveness entails. It is a contentious matter, subject to different interpretations, often ideologically charged. One such effort is the Global Competitiveness Index, which measures 12 'pillars': institutions; infrastructure; macroeconomic environment; health and primary education; higher education and training; goods market efficiency; labour market efficiency; financial market development; technological readiness; market size; business sophistication; and innovation.

Small countries, including the Nordics, are prominent here, taking the top five places, but so are some larger countries such as Germany, the United Kingdom and the United States, which can mobilise large resources and have large financial markets and research bases. What we can say is that large size does not seem to confer any particular advantage in itself and that having a large public sector does not seem in itself to carry penalties. Indeed the table would appear to confirm the idea that the size of the public sector itself is irrelevant.

It is now widely accepted that purely economic measures do not capture human wellbeing adequately. We need, rather, to incorporate broader measures of life experiences, including of social wellbeing, health and satisfaction. One such is the United Nations Human Development Index. This measures gross national income (GNI) per capita, the usual yardstick for economic prosperity, but also takes into health and education, in the form of life expectancy at birth and years of schooling. Again, large and wealthy countries like the United States and Germany feature high in the ranking but so do small states, including the Nordic countries, characterised by social investment. The United Kingdom comes in at number 26. An even broader measure of wellbeing is the Happiness Index, also published by the United Nations (Helliwell, Layard and Sachs, 2013). This looks at GDP per capita but also social support: healthy life expectancy; freedom to make life choices; generosity; and corruption. In this case, small European states take the top five places.

We can conclude that small states, even without large natural resources, can be as competitive in world markets as large ones, if they are organised appropriately. Moreover, the more broadly development is defined to include social dimensions, the clearer their advantage. There is strong evidence that small European states with open economies might better respond to the challenges of global markets but do so in different ways. Transitional economies might be tempted to the 'low road' of market liberalism, but mature welfare states can thrive through the 'high road' of social investment. Of course, noting that the top ranks in the index are dominated by small states does not mean that all small states do well. Many small countries do not make it into the top 20 in any of these indices. To succeed, a small country needs to organise itself properly.

Table 4.2 – Indices of Wellbeing			
Rank	Global competitiveness	Human Development	Happiness
1	Switzerland	Norway	Denmark
2	Singapore	Australia	Norway
3	Finland	United States	Switzerland
4	Sweden	Netherlands	Netherlands
5	Netherlands	Germany	Sweden
6	Germany	New Zealand	Canada
7	United States	Sweden	Finland
8	United Kingdom	Ireland	Austria
9	Hong Kong	Switzerland	Iceland
10	Japan	Japan	Australia
11	Qatar	Canada	Israel
12	Denmark	South Korea	Costa Rica
13	Taiwan	Hong Kong	New Zealand
14	Canada	Iceland	UAE
15	Norway	Denmark	Panama
16	Austria	Israel	Mexico
17	Belgium	Belgium	United States
18	Saudi Arabia	Austria	Ireland
19	South Korea	Singapore	Luxembourg
20	Australia	France	Venezuela

Sources: World Economic Forum, *The Global Competitiveness Index 2012–2013*, Geneva: World Economic Forum.
United Nations Development Project, *Human Development Report 2013*, New York: United Nations.
Helliwell, Layard and Sachs (2013).

CHAPTER 5

Adapting to Change

Strategy

MARKET LIBERAL AND social investment strategies are not merely clusters of policies adopted at will and changed easily. They are long-term trajectories, built into the institutions of government and society and with an internal coherence such that changing one element will have effects on the others. Governments, moreover, cannot just assume that policies will be carried out exactly in the form in which they were designed. Everything that we know about public policy making suggests that it is a slow process and that change often proceeds in small steps, albeit with occasional sharp breaks in continuity. Small states are particularly constrained in what they can do and, as we have stressed, need to be flexible and adapt to external change. If the market liberal strategy merely involves taking whatever the international market place dictates, then in a way this is the easier, if not the best, strategy. Social investment, and its social democratic variant, requires a great deal more by way of institutions and social practices. The trick is to structure policy-making processes such as to produce positive-sum outcomes rather than mutually destructive competition, while retaining international competitiveness.

Corporatism

In the 1980s, Katzenstein (1985) identified the secret of adaptation of small states to global markets as corporatism. This is essentially a mode of policy making in which government, business and trade unions get together to thrash out agreements on long-term goals and commitments (Schmitter, 1974). The idea is that, with cooperation, they can achieve more than through competition or conflict. Unions can accept wage restraint and thus contain inflation and business costs, in return for full employment and increases in real wages. They may also accept lower individual wages increases in return for increases in the 'social wage' in the form of public services such as health and education, which directly benefit their members. Business commits to investment in the knowledge that markets will expand, wages will be under control and infrastructure provided. Government agrees to fund public services and expand infrastructure, in the knowledge that the other partners will deliver their part of the bargain. Corporatism may be used in good times to avoid booms getting out of control, and at times of crisis or external shocks, in order to recover production levels without going through massive unemployment. Corporatism was not confined to small states but it has often been argued that they are particularly good at it because of their short lines of communication, the trust among key actors and their shared commitment to national progress. In its classic form, however, it depended on certain preconditions.

One is the existence of national capital, that is domestically-owned businesses that had a stake in the prosperity of the country and were unable to relocate easily. Locked in by national boundaries, they had a strong incentive to cooperate with the other social partners to produce public goods from which all could benefit. While neo-liberal economists tend to regard all firms as behaving in much the same way in accordance with a single capitalist logic, sociologists have often drawn attention to different models of capitalism (Hall and Soskice, 2001). In liberal market economies, firms compete with each other according to individualistic market principles. They typically aim to maximise profits in the short term and, nowadays, the value of their shares. Governments take a hands-off approach, leaving the market to itself. In coordinated market economies, on the other hand, business is organised in associations, which regulate their own affairs and cooperate (as well as competing) to produce public goods from which they can all benefit, such as skilled labour. Firms look to the long term and often aim at increasing market share and expanding production, rather than maximising profit in the short term. Such firms are more likely to be amenable to corporatist bargaining and collective action.

A second condition is the existence of strong and centralised associations representing business and labour. These can control their own members and come to agreements, knowing that they can deliver. If business firms can opt out of associations, on the other hand, they can just free ride by enjoying the benefits negotiated by the associations without paying the dues. If trade unions do not cover the work force, they similarly will be unable to deliver and if they are not strong enough they may be undermined by shop-floor militancy. The broader the coverage of unions, moreover, the more they overlap with society and so have an incentive to focus on the social wage rather than just the sectoral interests of their own members. The bargains that emerge from corporatism and other forms of concerted action, of course, will often depend on the weight of the various interests so that we might get more business-oriented corporatism focused on economic development in the narrow sense or more socially-oriented versions, where trade union and other social interests are stronger. Figure 5.1 shows that the Nordic states have high rates of trade union membership and the Baltics have low levels, with the UK and Ireland in between.

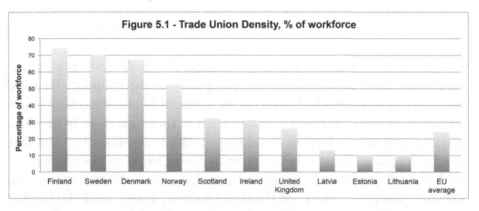

Figure 5.1 - Trade Union Density, % of workforce

Corporatism may also require a sense of common national interest and shared institutional framework such that all accept the legitimacy of the political arena. It is this that sustains a degree of trust and allows groups to lose some rounds of bargaining in the knowledge that they can win in the future. As we explain later, this does not necessarily stem from ethnicity or exclusive cultural ties, but often from shared experiences or moments of crisis when everyone was forced to pull together in the face of an external threat.

Finally, corporatism needs a strong government, able to tax and spend effectively and to deliver on its commitments. This does not need to be single-party government or beyond challenge. Indeed, corporatist arrangements are often combined with proportional representation, which ensures that a wide spectrum of political opinion is incorporated in decisions. There does, however, need to be an effective administration.

The central feature of corporatist bargaining has often been national wage negotiations, conducted by employers and unions, sometimes with a role for the state. This secures a basic agreement on the distribution of the social product, with universal trade unionism ensuring that wage differentials are not excessive. On top of this are built a variety of other elements, including the 'social wage', commitments to public investment and measures to meet the needs of particular groups within the community.

The downside of corporatism, even when it has been effective as policy, is the way in which it downgrades parliamentary institutions and thus, according to some, can undermine democracy. This is an objection heard from both right and left, with political parties complaining about deals being struck by powerful interests remote from everyday citizen concerns. It is also centralising, putting power in the hands of business and union leaders and potentially discouraging participation and pluralism. Small business groups, the self-employed, non-unionised workers, consumers, the unemployed and the retired can all feel left out.

The United Kingdom made sporadic efforts at corporatism under both Conservative and Labour governments in the 1960s and 1970s. Although it was linked at various times to national economic planning, industrial policy and welfare state expansion, it came to be identified essentially with wage bargaining and incomes policy, seeking to limit wage and price increases at a time of rising inflation. It actually proved reasonably successful in this at a time of massive external inflationary pressures, and at a much lower cost in unemployment and destruction of industrial capacity than what followed in the 1980s, but it ultimately broke down. The failure to enforce a government-backed wage limit in 1979 led to the wave of strikes known as the 'winter of discontent' (1978–9) and ushered in the Thatcher government, which was determined to remove all traces of corporatism. Although hostile commentators usually blamed this on excessive trade union power, it is arguable that the failure of British corporatism resulted from the weakness of all three parties, who were unable to arrive at, or deliver on, binding commitments. It was not leadership intransigence but grass-roots militancy that undermined wage policy. The unions, true to their historic fear of state interference, had turned down offers in the 1960s that would have recognised them legally as a regulated part of the public domain. Employers are weakly organised – although they had, with government encouragement, formed their own body, the Confederation of British Industry, in the early 1960s, this never established itself as the authoritative voice of business.

By the 1980s it was widely held that corporatism was on the way out everywhere, as a result of globalisation and the opening of markets (Jones, 2008). The very idea of national capitalism made little sense in a world dominated by global corporations and mobile investment. Capital, it was said, had no homeland and no incentive to engage in bargaining within it. Trade unions were in decline, a process that has continued apace, especially in the private sector and in multinational corporations. The very complexity of the economy and of employment markets made the old bargains increasing irrelevant. The spiralling costs of the welfare state meant that government could not continually increase the social wage but rather sought containment and retrenchment. Corporatism looked like a recipe for good times, when it meant agreeing on how to share out an expanding cake, unsuited to the austerity brought on by the global oil crises. Economic problems in coordinated market or corporatist states such as Germany and Sweden were attributed to the sclerosis brought on by having to negotiate change and allowing declining sectors a veto on innovation. Post-reunification Germany was even represented as the 'sick man of Europe'. From being the secret of success, corporatism became the scapegoat for failure. It was neo-liberal economics, as practised in the United States and the United Kingdom, that became the accepted wisdom. In Sweden, often seen as the archetype of the corporatist small state, the formula was officially abandoned when employers pulled out in the mid-1980s.

Corporatism was never confined to small states but was particularly important to them, given their need to adjust to global markets without provoking excessive social divisions or unsustainable levels of unemployment. In its strong form it has proved most enduring in Norway, in Belgium and in Austria. In Sweden it has largely been abandoned in favour of market adjustment, although the continuing strength of trade unions means that the underlying ideas of compromise have not totally been abandoned. The Netherlands moved from corporatism, which was linked to older traditions of accommodation between religious communities (known as consociationalism) to a looser form of co-ordination labelled the 'Polder Model' from the Dutch tradition of cooperation in the common enterprise of reclaiming land and keeping out the sea. Ireland moved towards concerted action in the 1980s but dramatically abandoned it in the fact of the economic crisis of the late 2000s. The experience of the transition states of eastern and central Europe has been highly diverse. The Baltic states embarked on a market liberal strategy from the outset, especially in Estonia. Slovenia, in contrast, practised neo-corporatism with a significant role for trade unions (Bohle and Greskovits, 2013). In the

Visegrad countries (Poland, Hungary, Czech Republic and Slovakia), social concertation was tried several times but never quite worked out and was eventually abandoned.

From Corporatism to Concerted Action

In the 1990s, however, a strange thing happened. In an effort to regain competitiveness and to qualify for the single European currency, a number of European states came back to negotiation among the social partners. Far from globalisation and internalisation of the economy destroying corporatism, it was argued, they could actually stimulate what Martin Rhodes (2002) called 'competitive corporatism'. This was not, for the most part, the fully corporatism of old, with binding agreements among peak groups. It was, rather, 'lean corporatism' (Traxler, 2004), 'social concertation' (Compston, 2002), 'social pacts' (Avdagic, Rhodes and Visser, 2011), 'social dialogue' or 'social partnership'. The European Commission was keen on the idea, buying into the idea of the social investment state and the new economic theories (noted above) that emphasise human capital, research and entrepreneurship as the key to economic success. It also diffused the idea (backed by Structural Funds moneys) at the local and regional level, where it sought to mobilise social forces to encourage development.

Wage negotiation often remains at the core of these social bargains, as they are focused on sustaining international competitiveness and maintaining real wages as opposed to inflationary wage increases that would leave workers no better off. They can provide business with knowledge of future costs, thus encouraging investment. Training and active labour market policy are key ingredients, again linked to competitiveness. In some cases, they have gone beyond individual wages in order to secure the social wage and maintain public services and welfare. There have been pressures to avoid the old corporatist insider deals by extending partnership to other groups, including social interests, the voluntary sector and environmentalists. In the modern world, however, it is business interests who have had the biggest say, while unions occupy a less powerful position than in the heyday of corporatism. It may also be that nowadays trade unions are on the back foot, weakened by loss of membership and bargaining power as well as the mobility of capital. In that case, concerted action may become just a means of delivering wage restraint rather than a genuine social compromise. Social and environmental interests come still further behind.

Large business and multinational firms tend to stand aside from social partnerships negotiated at national level, preferring to deal directly with governments. They are increasingly able to offer, or to withhold, investment. On the other hand, they do benefit from wage stability, public services and trained manpower, even where they do not participate actively in concertation. In some countries, vocational training is entrusted to partnerships of employers and unions, with the former having to pay levies to finance it. This provides a disincentive to free riding and a strong motive for getting involved. Small businesses are often not organised in effective associations – sometimes they have to work within bodies dominated by the big firms, and are unable to make their voices heard. It is medium-sized enterprises that often have the most to gain from social concertation, tied as they are into the national system and needing support that big firms can provide for themselves. Accordingly it works most effectively where there is such tier of firms, what the Germans call the *Mittelstand*.

Social concertation also differs from classic corporatism in being more flexible. There is scope to change plans if external circumstances change and, if an issue is blocked in one negotiating forum, it can be taken out and dealt with somewhere else. Rather than a single set of peak negotiations trying to resolve everything around the same table, there may be multiple venues for concertation and negotiation. This reduces veto points and blockages, while providing incentives for cooperation. Sometimes it is very lightly institutionalised indeed but even where formal partnership bodies have been disbanded, the idea of negotiation and compromise persists. Not all firms may engage in national-level bargaining, but others may abide by its outcomes. Where a crisis hits, there may still be a tendency to organise a summit or social partnership. In this way, the shadow of corporatism survives its formal demise. Consensus is sought as far as possible and stark clashes between labour and capital avoided. These attitudes and practices become embedded in the national culture, where culture is understood as learned behaviour rather than ethnicity. Such learning is facilitated by what Milner (2013) calls political literacy, a widespread knowledge and understanding of politics and public affairs.

Institutionalising Cooperation

The mechanisms for corporatism, lean corporatism and social partnership vary greatly. The original design for corporatism, in the early 20th century, envisaged the replacement of parliamentary institutions by bodies representing occupational groups. In practice, this was implemented almost exclusively in Fascist states such as Spain and Italy, where the groups were subordinated to the state. This experience and the concern for democracy have since discredited that idea. Instead, corporatist institutions have existed alongside parliamentary ones. In the heyday of corporatism, there were often very formal institutions representing the social partners, whose decisions were, in practice if not in law, binding on the participants. As this form of rigid corporatism became more difficult, and especially after concertation was revived in the 1990s, social pacts came into fashion. These are periodic agreements, typically covering a limited range of issues and aimed specifically at adjustment to change. As these pacts have no constitutional standing, they can be used by governments as convenient and abandoned at will.

Another common mechanism for bringing in the social partners is the social and economic council. These exist in such diverse countries as Italy, Spain, France, Ireland, Greece and Finland but not in the Scandinavian countries or Germany, where corporatism has historically been stronger. They are also widespread in eastern and central Europe, including Slovenia, Croatia, Hungary, the Czech Republic, Poland, Slovakia and Romania. In the United Kingdom, a National Economic Development Council (Neddy) was set up in 1962 along with sectoral councils for particular industries (Little Neddies) and, after 1964, regional economic planning councils. The regional councils were abolished and Neddy was sidelined by the Thatcher Government after 1979. Neddy was abolished in 1992 and nothing like it has been proposed since. Economic and social councils are typically serviced by agencies providing research and data. They are not, by and large, forums for tripartite negotiation and thrashing out social compromises, but do serve to find common ground in social and economic development, taking long term policy issues out of confrontational party politics, and for diffusing ideas about good policy. They have thus facilitated social dialogue, compromise and long-term thinking.

Below these peak bodies there is often a dense network of bodies providing places for social cooperation. In some countries, management of training and active labour market policies is devolved to the social partners, with government playing a larger or smaller role depending on the case. Social partners including trade unions may manage social assistance and unemployment benefits. Local economic development partnerships have been encouraged by the European Commission, which has sought to make these inclusive of labour and social interests, as well as business, encountering some stiff opposition from British Conservative governments in the process.

Cultures of Concertation

We have already discussed the ideas of Alesina and Spoloare (2003), who argue that in small states people will tend to agree because their populations are more homogeneous. As we also noted, this is an elusive notion, which is impossible to define, let alone measure. Nations are socially stratified societies, with rich and poor, employers and workers and a host of other divisions. Social concertation and negotiation happens, not because everyone has the same preferences and interests but precisely because they do not, and must therefore arrive at positive-sum compromises.

Some years ago, there was a debate on 'social capital' as the key ingredient that explained social cooperation, especially in small societies. It was popularised (but not invented) by Robert Putnam (1993) in a study of Italian regions, which purported to show differences in both economic and social performance, which Putnam attributed to differences in social capital. Unfortunately, having declared that it was social capital that facilitated cooperation, he then defined social capital in a circular way, as that thing which facilitated cooperation. He then measured social capital by examining differences in attitudes and degrees of trust among citizens of Italian regions as revealed in surveys and to associationalism, or members of associations of all sorts. These in turn were attributed to social and economic patterns set down hundreds of years before, notably the differences between feudal and non-feudal regions.

Putnam's work has been cited so often and taken up by policy makers as the key to explaining the performance of societies that it is worth taking a moment to point out its shortcomings. Social capital is not, in fact, an attribute of individuals that can be measured in surveys asking them about attitudes. It is, rather, a set of relationships among individuals in a specific social context. Membership of associations is no guarantee that people will engage in virtuous cooperation. The south of Italy is rife with associations, including those with criminal intent. Other scholars have noted that the proliferation of associations can merely produce deadlock and problems in cooperating beyond their limit. Putnam later sought to correct this with a somewhat contrived distinction between 'bonding social capital' and 'bridging social capital' but it is not clear how we would know in advance which is which. The sharp north-south divide in Italy is not something that goes back to the Middle Ages, and in any case historians tend to argue that feudalism is the precursor of modern capitalism. Italy's persistent division is the result, rather, of the way that the country was unified in the 19th century, creating an artificial single market of very different economies, breaking links with the outside, and creating a permanent disadvantage for the south. Putnam's focus on cultural differences was merely repeating an old stereotype, already popularised in the 1950s by the work of Banfield (1958).

A different, and more sociologically informed idea of trust rejects both essentialist arguments based on shared ethnicity, which privilege the community over the individual, and individualist accounts, which look only at the attitudes of individuals. Instead, they look at relationships, examining what Sabel (1993) calls 'studied trust'. This refers to the emergence of effective common purposes and trust as a result of experience. As so often, Alexis de Tocqueville (1986: 230) spotted this in the 19th century (even if he did use the gendered language of the times):

> There is another (love of country) more rational than this (blind loyalty); less generous, perhaps less ardent but more fecund and more durable; this one is born of the enlightenment; it develops with the help of laws, it grows with the exercise of rights and finishes by somehow becoming identical with personal interests. A man understands the influence which the wellbeing of the country has on his own: he knows that the law permits him to contribute to producing this wellbeing, and he concerns himself with the prosperity of his country, first as something which is useful to him, and then as his own work.

This suggests that social capital and trust can be built and that institutions and practice have a big role to play. It is not necessary for everyone to share the same beliefs and values as long as they share the same political space and can engage in compromises and cooperation in pursuit of mutual shared interests. Trust matters because actors may need to accept painful things in the short term with the knowledge that they will pay off in the longer term. Otherwise, everyone may seek short-term advantage, to the mutual harm of all.

The same constructivist approach can be applied to notions of national character and culture, which are so often invoked to explain political outcomes. Nations are said to be marked by historic patterns and naturally inclined to entrepreneurship, to individualism or collectivism, or whatever. Politicians and nation-builders certainly use these stylised images in order to mobilise the populations behind their favoured projects but they rarely survive serious scrutiny. Indeed, they are usually no more than stereotypes. We can see this from the way in which the stereotypes can change rapidly according to need. Orson Welles' lines from *The Third Man* (1949) are well known:

> Harry Lime: Don't be so gloomy. After all it's not that awful. Like the fella says, in Italy for 30 years under the Borgias they had warfare, terror, murder, and bloodshed, but they produced Michelangelo, Leonardo da Vinci, and the Renaissance. In Switzerland they had brotherly love – they had 500 years of democracy and peace, and what did that produce? The cuckoo clock.

In fact, before the civil war of 1848, Switzerland was marked by murderous warfare and civil strife – the transition to peace and harmony was quite rapid (Steinberg, 1996). Germany was known before the 19th century as a land of scholars and musicians before being identified with militarism and then economic miracles and peace. The Irish pub was at one time the symbol of backwardness (think of male-dominated drinking dens) but with the Celtic Tiger in the 1990s became the ultimate in cosmopolitan post-modern chic, springing up in every city in Europe.

Indeed, the national stereotypes that are invoked to explain success and failure of social projects are usually merely rationalisations of the outcome rather than real causes. It is striking to observe how often it is exactly the same qualities that are invoked to account for success at one time and place and for failure at another (Keating, 2008; Keating, Loughlin and Deschouwer, 2003). So individualism can be presented as an entrepreneurial virtue to explain success, or as a lack of social capital and cooperation, to explain failure. Collectivism and a sense of community can be presented as social capital or as a lack of entrepreneurial spirit. A strong sense of tradition can be spun as evidence of being trapped in the past, or as the basis for community and social capital. Cultural homogeneity can be invoked to explain common purpose, but cultural diversity can equally be used to explain innovation. It is not, therefore, these embedded cultural characteristics of society that explain the capacity for adaptation but the way that cultural images and traditions are pressed into the service to underpin a particular development project.

The past does matter, since it leaves a legacy of policies and institutions to a nation, which cannot always be changed overnight. What also matters, however, is the way this past is portrayed and used to sustain visions of the present and the future. This takes us into the realm of ideas.

The Battle of Ideas

Ideas as well as interests are important in politics. Indeed it is ideas that tell us what our interests are and with whom we share them. Some ideas are explicitly articulated and challenged while others are implicit, tacitly accepted at any time as the 'received wisdom'. In recent years, there has been a dramatic shift in received wisdom towards the liberal market economy or, in the term used by its critics, 'neo-liberalism'. This contains a number of distinct elements, emphasised variously at different times and places. One is the idea that the state should intervene as little as possible in the market economy. While this is central to neo-liberalism, it is not always practised. Ostensibly market liberal governments, such as those of Reagan in the United States and Thatcher in the United Kingdom, have offered massive state support and protection for the arms industry. UK privatisation programmes have produced numerous monopolies and cartels. Another element in the neo-liberal prospectus has been monetarism, the idea that control of the money supply and interest rates is an objective science and the key to macroeconomic stability. Experience under the Thatcher government showed that the very definition of money and money supply was elusive, let alone its control. In 1997, the Blair/ Brown government continued on the monetarist road by giving operational independence to the Bank of England, another idea that was spreading as part of received wisdom and which, during the boom of the early 2000s, looked like a success. The global crisis starting in 2008, however, led to much of the monetarist rule book being ripped up as central banks and governments resorted to measures such as quantitative easing (in effect, printing money).

Another strand of neo-liberalism has been to identify the interests of business and business leaders with that of the country. This is something which the Scottish economist and philosopher Adam Smith (often wrongly invoked as a neo-liberal) warned against in the eighteenth century. Yet, as we wrote this chapter, the heads of 24 of the largest UK companies responded thus to a proposal from Labour's Shadow Chancellor to a proposal to raise the marginal rate of income tax on those earning over £150,000 by five pence in the pound (to 50 per cent):

> We are concerned to see Ed Balls and the Labour Party calling for higher taxes on businesses and business people. We think that these higher taxes will have the effect of discouraging business investment in the UK. This is a backwards step which would put the economic recovery at risk and would very quickly lead to the loss of jobs in Britain.
>
> *Daily Telegraph* (27 Jan. 2014)

This was accompanied by a cacophony of protests from business groups. It seems, to say the least, implausible that such a modest proposal could have such drastic consequences. Top rates of income tax had been 60 per cent in 1988, nine years into Margaret Thatcher's term and we have noted high marginal rates in successful countries. Balls had not proposed increases in taxes on business, nor had he singled out business people among those earning more than £150,000. Yet the received wisdom of the times is that, in an era of globalisation, mildly progressive taxation is just not possible. So the wealthy can present self-interest in the garb of national welfare, while the claims of labour are dismissed as sectional. In a small state, with a restricted tax base, this kind of threat of a flight of investors can be even more powerful.

All of this provides the ideological backdrop for the rejection of social concertation and partnership in favour of a particular idea of the market economy. Social concertation, if it is to be accepted nowadays, can be sold more easily as an effective mode of economic management, rather than a broader mode of social accommodation.

From Corporatism to Governance?

The early globalisation literature was replete with references to the retreat of the state in the face of the market, a prospect greeted with hope or fear depending on the political perspective of the observer. Nowadays the general consensus is that, without a state and system of law, markets simply cannot work. More recently, there has been a debate about a supposed shift from 'government' to 'governance'. This latter term has been given a bewildering variety of meanings but usually it is deployed to suggest that there has been a shift from an old world in which public policy was made by states, which then carried it out unilaterally, to a world in which policy is negotiated by myriad groups in networks. Arguably, this is just the old debate about corporatism and social concertation dressed up in new language. Certainly the idea that in the past governments made policy without reference to powerful social and economic actors is rather farfetched and has been advanced only to be able to claim that the world has changed. The term governance, however, has been taken up and deployed by states and international institutions such as the World Bank, International Monetary Fund and European Union, in a way that is highly significant. It has allowed them to bring back ideas of cooperation and partnership while seeming to remain faithful to neo-liberal ideas and rejecting 'old-fashioned' ideas of corporatism. To do this, some further relabeling is necessary. So private groups, which might be condemned as 'interest groups' or even 'special interests' can be relabelled 'social partners' or, better still, simply part of 'civil society'. 'Subsidiarity', a doctrine dear to the European Commission, legitimises the involvement of groups, including business and trade unions, in shaping and delivery policy within their own spheres.

The language of governance tends to be rather depoliticised, suggesting that groups in society will come to agreement on the common good if only they talk to each other, and that problems have objectively correct solutions. The truth is rather that in a modern society, public policy is always going to be negotiated among interests and compromises reached. The interesting questions concern the power of different groups, who gets what and the effectiveness of institutions. Modern forms of concerted action tend to give the bigger role to business rather than unions, while other social interests may be marginalised. Concerted action can produce positive-sum compromises, which enhance growth and therefore provide more resources for distribution. On the other hand, it might encourage rent-seeking, that is groups each seeking to enlarge their share of the cake at the expense of others without increasing the overall size of the pie. The design of institutions is therefore critical, as is the role of government as guardian of the general interest.

The Importance of Government

Market liberals and proponents of corporatism or governance often tend to downplay the role of government in the old-fashioned sense. Modern states, especially small states, may have lost some of the macroeconomic change and security but they remain key actors in public policy and, in some respects, may have become even more important. It is in these respects that small states may be particularly relevant. The modern economy is highly dependent on public goods furnished by states, of which the most important is probably the rule of law, without which markets cannot operate. They also provide education, training and infrastructure, essential to business as well as citizens. Social protection contributes not only to the welfare of beneficiaries but to social stability. Governments are also, even in the most market liberal of states, responsible for managing a large amount of money in taxes and public expenditure.

The state is also a key actor in social concertation, providing the necessary forums and holding the ring between capital, labour and other interests. Social concertation, even when government is formally absent, may take place in the 'shadow of hierarchy', that is in the knowledge that government may intervene and does expect results. To do this, government needs a degree of independence from those interests and an ability to articulate a general, public interest that goes beyond them. Government also provides democratic legitimacy for social compromises – the role of parliaments is crucial here.

Governments of small states do not have the same policy capacity as large ones. They employ fewer people, have fewer resources for research and have small administrative apparatuses. It is therefore particularly important that they be able to target resources and focus on strategic issues. Small size may be an advantage in that they can make connections among different policy fields more easily and identify key issues across departments. On the other hand, they might more easily be captured by private interests, which may have more information and capacity than they do and in a smaller society the interests may not be numerous enough to balance each other out. Small societies might also be prone to clientelism or to powerful interest groups effectively colonising parts of the governmental apparatus. Various mechanisms are available to overcome this tendency. One is to organise government by policy tasks rather than by traditional functional areas, in which entrenched interests may be too powerful.

68

Another is a small cabinet focused on key policy areas and with the ability to discuss policy genuinely and to arrive at conclusions. This form of coordination may be more effective than having a powerful prime minister's department which could become too dominant, or a ministry of finance that determines financial allocations and gets too heavily involved in policy matters, so stifling innovation across government as a whole. Since civil servants in small governments will generally have a broader range of responsibilities than those in large ones, they may lack specialist knowledge but be able to link up discrete policy fields – this requires a different order of skills.

Small governments need to be innovative, since they cannot afford to carry the dead weight of old policies. They also need to be able to terminate old programmes that have outlived their usefulness in order to free up resources for new ones. All of this suggests that small-state governments are not merely large-state ones at a reduced scale but need qualitatively different structures and skills.

Playing the European Game

In a world of independent nation-states, there are, as we have seen, some advantages to being large. Big states, able to throw their weight around, can do well at time of international anarchy. Small states, on the other hand, have a strong interest in international law and in limits on the ability of states to act unilaterally. This would suggest that small states should favour European integration. On the other hand, small states have often had to struggle for their independence, which they guard jealously, and might be suspicious of international bodies dominated by their historic opponents. So while some Danes might see the European Union as a way of securing their independence, others will evoke memories of German hegemony. In Belgium, where the great powers had been accustomed to fight their wars, there is a broad consensus on the need for Europe. For the Baltic states, the range of Euro-Atlantic institutions (the European Union, NATO, the Organisation for Cooperation and Security in Europe and the Council of Europe) can be seen to bolster their newly-found independence, but their reliance on these institutions jostles with a concern for sovereignty. In Norway, Sweden and Finland, the northern peripheral areas are suspicious of a European project that seems to benefit the south and threaten their national territorial settlements.

The result is a variety of strategies with regard to Europe. Norway and Iceland have debated joining the EU on various occasions, but in the end have stayed out. They do, however, need the internal European market for economic reasons and so have signed up to association agreements under the European Economic Area. The result is that they have to accept European single market rules without having any say in how those rules are made, and must contribute to the EU budget. Denmark joined along with the United Kingdom in 1973, being highly dependent on British markets, but has secured various opt-outs. It is not obliged to participate in European defence cooperation, although it is a member of NATO, which imposes rather more onerous obligations and includes most of the same states. It has an opt-out from the Euro single currency but it pegs its own currency to it so that it loses control of its own monetary policy without gaining a say over the wider European policy. Sweden does not have an opt-out from the Euro but in practice has not joined and would need a referendum in order to do so.

There is therefore a trade-off between retaining national sovereignty and influencing European policy. Countries such as Norway and Iceland risk ending up with the worst of both worlds. It is for this reason, that the Scottish National Party has embraced Europe since the 1980s, as an essential framework for independence. Small states, however, do not enjoy the same influence within Europe as do larger ones.

Policy making in the European Union follows two modes. The classic one is the community method, which is intended to privilege the wider European interest at each stage over the interests of member states. So the European Commission has the sole right to initiate policy proposals across most fields. These must be taken through national governments, the Committee of Permanent Representatives (which represents member states in Brussels) and the Council of the European Union (also known as the Council of Ministers), which represents the national governments. Gradually the role of the European Parliament has been enhanced so that it has co-decision rights across most policy fields. It is organised on the basis of cross-national party groups in order to downplay the role of national interests. There is a complex process of *engrenage* (gearing) by which these various states are expected to lead to a result that is more than the sum of national preferences, but represents a gain in integration. The metaphor of the bicycle has been employed to suggest that Europe can only remain in being if it keeps on moving forward.

The other mode of policy making is the intergovernmental one, in which states bargain with each other and make trade-offs among their interests. There may be package deals, by which one state gets something in one field and another state gets something in a different field. Deals are also struck outside the formal procedures, so that decisions in the Council are sometimes effectively taken in advance. In recent decades, the European Council, a meeting of heads of government, which operates largely in inter-governmental mode, has been formalised and recognised in the treaties.

In order to remove blockages in the system and allow some flexibility, other procedures have emerged in recent years. One is the Open Method of Coordination, whereby states agree to pursue common policy goals but outside the community method and without imposing formal or binding legislation. Another is Enhanced Cooperation, which allows groups of states to go ahead on their own where it is not possible to reach general agreement on a policy field.

Large states have greater economic weight so that their consent to policy measures is more important. They have greater policy capacity, so can prepare policies across the whole range of relevant issues and be present wherever policy is being made. They have more voting power in the Council of the European Union under the majority-voting provisions, which now apply to most areas of policy making. Until 2014 each state has had a fixed number of votes and while smaller states have proportion ately more votes in relation to their population than do large ones, the latter still predominate. As of November 2014, a qualified majority will consist of 55 per cent of member states covering 65 per cent of the population, which still favours big states.

In those fields still subject to unanimity, all states possess a veto on decisions, which appears to give small states an advantage, since they can threaten to hold matters up unless they gain concessions, even in unrelated fields. In practice, small states rarely use, or threaten to use, the veto. They need friends among other states and can easily be isolated and marginalised. Small states find it more difficult to make side-deals outside the formal decision-making process as they have less to offer in return. It is for this reason that small states have more to gain from the community method than from intergovernmental bargaining. Under the community method, there is a premium on finding common ground across a broad range of interests and the role of the Commission helps to ensure that the European aspects are stressed and not just those of the big players.

In some ways, the EU has become friendlier to small states. Successive enlargements have meant that they are now in the majority and able to resist treaty changes that would reduce their influence. The weakening of the old Franco-German axis has encouraged a more pluralist politics, with shifting alliances. On the other hand, there has been a rise in inter-governmentalism (including the emergence of the European Council) and a weakening of the Commission since its high point in the 1990s.

Small states can exercise real influence within the EU, but not in the same way as large states (Panke, 2010). Rather than throwing their weight about, they form alliances with other states to achieve majorities. They do often end up on the winning side since their strategy is to extract concessions from the majority coalition rather than being pushed into the minority. Their lack of 'hard power' in the form of economic weight and votes may be compensated by 'soft power', which depends more on influencing policy development through good ideas. Following the community method, they achieve more by contributing to positive outcomes, using knowledge and experience and showing how their ideas can contribute to Europe as a whole rather than just a national interest. This effect is enhanced where small states have a reputation for being constructive and pro-European rather than engaging in combat and emerging from meetings constantly claiming to have scored a victory against Europe, as tends to the case with the UK government.

It is important for small states to get into the policy process at the beginning in order to shape choices. Positive relations with the European Commission (in developing policy initiatives) and in the Committee of Permanent Representatives (CORPER) are crucial. Networking in Brussels is also crucial. This includes knowing one's way around the institutions, having co-nationals working there and a command of languages. In recent years, the number of UK nationals entering the institutions has seriously declined. In 2009 the UK Government (but not the Scottish Government) abolished its scholarships for the College of Europe, an important feeder for the European institutions. Small states need to build a capacity in Brussels and within the home-based ministries to enable them to engage with European policy matters, to identify the opportunities for informing policy in the early stages, and for anticipating upcoming issues. Enhanced capacity also helps ensure national governments can work closely with delegations in Brussels and the Council of the EU to facilitate influence through networking.

Small states can overcome weaknesses resulting from limited resources by building niche expertise in key policy fields, and gaining a reputation for policy leadership, scientific and technical knowledge. For example, Denmark has taken a lead on wind energy, climate change mitigation and 'flexicurity' in labour markets. Sweden has been able to shape norms underpinning European defence and security policies. Older small states tend to be more effective than newer ones. They have more experience and have developed networks and institutions to deal with EU matters.

So it seems that small states can be most effective when they are most integrated into the EU and its institutions and are seen to be positive players. Joining the Union represents a loss of sovereignty and autonomy to do things on their own, but the benefit is increased influence at the European level. Once again, we see that effectiveness in the external sphere depends on how a nation is organised internally.

Variations

Small states can therefore develop strategies to manage vulnerabilities and forge their own development projects within an interlinked world. This is not because they are cultural monoliths in which everyone thinks the same way. Rather they are political communities, in which ideas are thrashed out and common interests must be forged. Their small size and short lines of communication may give them an advantage in concerted action and planning for change. Their very vulnerability in world markets may stimulate cooperation and discourage complacency. They cannot do some of the things that large states can do, but may be better than their bigger neighbours at others. There is no single recipe and how they respond to global challenges differs from one case to another so that generalisations about largeness or smallness in general are unhelpful. The varieties of response are explored in the following chapters by examining the Nordic countries (close the social democratic/social investment model), the Baltic states (near to the market liberal pole) and Ireland (a hybrid model).

CHAPTER 6

The Nordic Zone. Social Democracy in Changing Times

The Historic Roots of the Nordic Model

DENMARK, NORWAY AND SWEDEN, which are social investment states with social democratic orientation, have, for several decades, provided something of a benchmark for proponents of a high tax, high spend model. Indeed, the 'Nordic Model' has been celebrated by social democrats as a successful means of combining economic growth with social assistance programmes. It has been lauded in other small polities such as Scotland as an attractive model to follow, and derided by neo-liberals as paternalist and anti-business. The Nordic Model, at least as a Weberian ideal-type, combines a comprehensive social security system with institutionalised social rights, social solidarity, and a tripartite bargaining system which requires co-operation between employers' associations, employees (organised through widespread unionisation) and the government. It requires high levels of taxation to provide for generous active labour market policies such as universal unemployment and sickness insurance, and correspondingly high levels of employment to ensure that revenue from taxation exceeds spending on welfare payments. It also requires high levels of social solidarity, which is achieved through universal programmes, ensuring that the middle classes receive the benefits they pay for through taxation. It is a social investment model that relies on human capital to provide social protection to citizens.

Pre-industrialism, the Nordic states functioned much like other European polities, although early universal suffrage and separate agrarian parties led to a much more egalitarian society. Some of the future principles which would underscore the Nordic model emerged at an early stage. Seven years of public education became the norm, introduced in Denmark in 1814, in Sweden in 1842 and in Norway in 1848. At the same time, Sweden and Norway began to provide basic medical services to the needy (Kildal and Kuhnle, 2005). These services were regulated by local authorities through national legislation passed in the mid-1800s and they remained selective in character. In the early 1900s, liberal governments in Denmark, Norway and Sweden introduced welfare programmes that provided better working conditions for employees in an attempt to overcome class conflict and create in its place a feeling of social solidarity (Brandal, Bratberg and Thorsen, 2013). Here was a first attempt to combine the principle of economic assistance with societal engineering.

It was only, however, with the emergence of trade unions affiliated to social democratic parties at the end of the 19th century that the principles of social democracy came to the fore in the Nordic states. Church and state bureaucracies began to merge at the turn of the century, creating a more efficient system of state assistance and helping to facilitate a protestant work ethic on a wider scale. Experience of two world wars helped to forge social cohesion (Brandal, Bratberg and Thorsen, 2013). After the Second World War, these conditions provided the basis for a distinct Nordic model of social investment. Cross-border learning was key – when a practice was adopted in one Nordic state it was, with a short delay and minor adjustments for national peculiarities, adopted in another one. Universal pension schemes were adopted first in Sweden in 1948 and copied by Denmark and Norway in 1957. Universal sickness insurance was initiated by Sweden in 1955, followed by Norway in 1956 then Denmark in 1960. The Bismarckian principles informing much of post-war Europe's welfare systems were abandoned in favour of tax-financing of social security, while women – in much of Europe, seen as *consumers* of welfare – were regarded in the Nordic states as equal actors in the labour market (Christiansen and Markkola, 2006). So 'a truly distinct Nordic – and especially, Swedish – model came into being' in the postwar period (Esping-Andersen, 1996: 11), emphasising both the distinctive nature of the social investment model pursued by the Nordic states and the position of Sweden as a leader in policy development.

Nevertheless, within an overarching Nordic model there are differences in the development of welfare systems within and between the states, corresponding to the realities of global political economy and domestic macroeconomic policies. Indeed, these differences in both the policies adopted and the development of welfare models in each of the states has led Hilson (2008) to argue that there is 'no set path for the development of a Nordic welfare model, and no blueprint for how it should be constructed'. The differing reactions of the Nordic states to similar financial crises in the 1990s indicate that each has different perceptions as to how the model functions at an optimal level, and, more specifically, how the Nordic style of social investment state can be preserved while maintaining economic growth and competitiveness in global markets.

The 'Golden Age' of Social Democracy

The collective experience of the Second World War and the resultant social cohesion meant that a major expansion of welfare systems in its aftermath met with little resistance in the Nordic states. The interwar period saw a shift in the power balance of interests, with the lower classes gaining parliamentary representation. In Denmark, Norway and Sweden, this meant a decline in support for the liberal and conservative parties of the bourgeoisie and the rise of social democracy. As a means of popular-ising the principles of social democracy, and to take advantage of the pre-existing feelings of social solidarity resulting from the shared experi-ence of war, social democratic parties sloganised the principles they were attempting to deliver. The most popular of these was the Swedish *Folkhem* ('people's home'), which was later mimicked by social democrats in Norway (*Norge for folket*) and Denmark (*Danmark for folket*) (Christiansen and Markkola, 2006). These principles delivered social democratic majorities in Norway and Sweden in the 1950s and 1960s, allowing the social dem-ocratic parties there, with the broad alliances they had forged with trade unions and employers' associations, to deliver their own welfare system. At this stage, social democratic parties were reluctant to adopt universal-ism for the welfare state, preferring instead means-testing to target those who required most help. For social democrats, this was a means of pre-serving class solidarity and maintaining their working-class bases – a means to ensure that welfare did not become too expensive – and a means to retain consistency with historic party policy that those who could afford to look after themselves did not need the state to provide for them.

Party systems in Denmark and Finland were more complex, which meant more input and pressure from other parties, in particular, the social liberals, to deliver universalism. In Norway and Sweden too, internal party competition, and external pressure from the fact that neighbours were adopting universalism as a principle led to revisions of social democratic party policies. The metaphors continued to set the normative standard expected, but there was a gap between the expectation and the social reality. It fell to the social democratic parties, both in and out of power to fill the gap (Kettunen and Peterson, 2011). The public thus became much more accepting of collectivist solutions, which were seen as pragmatic and efficient. Redistributive taxation, state planning, public ownership of industry and wage bargaining all emerged as part of an extensive reform package aimed at delivering broad social democratic policies. The comprehensiveness of the welfare state was the key principle in the early postwar period. Universalism ensured that everyone, irrespective of levels of income tax or personal wealth, qualified for benefits. This tied the middle classes into the welfare system and provided the legitimacy the welfare state required through social solidarity – everyone paid into the system, and everyone benefited from it.

Perhaps the key feature of the Nordic Model of the 1950s and 1960s was an institutionalised system of wage negotiation through tripartite bargaining. Negotiations revisited on a regular basis helped reduce the tensions between employers and employees seen in other states. Central-isation of union organisation coupled with high levels of membership provided unions with a powerful voice in negotiations, while businesses were represented effectively by collective employers' associations. Succes-sive governments played a role in these discussions and incorporated the negotiations into broader macroeconomic policy. Involving the trade unions helped to contribute to wage restraint as the unions were able to accept wage limits on the understanding that the state would work with employers' associations to deliver full employment while providing welfare payments for those unemployed.

Political consensus played a role in maintaining the strength of the social investment model. Social democrats in Norway and Sweden spent long periods in office as majority governments until the late 1960s, but in the years afterwards majority governments were much rarer. Non-social democratic parties then became more involved in governing in several ways – as coalition partners to social democrats, by providing support to minority social democratic governments, and even leading non-social democratic coalitions. These complex political patterns led to wider coop-eration across ideological lines. Compromises over public policy were commonplace, with strong and centralised interest groups such as the trade unions and employers' associations facilitating this (Petersen and Åmark, 2006). Consequently, even in periods of government dominated by social democratic parties, liberal and conservative parties played a role in shaping welfare states. As a result of their public policy input while out of office, centre-right parties were also tied to the key principles of the welfare state and little attempt was made to dismantle it. (Christiansen and Markkola, 2006). Social democratic thinking thus extended beyond the social democratic parties, not only to other political parties, but also to society more widely. This was evidenced by public support for the welfare state remaining high even when support for social democratic parties fluctuated. In particular, the central tenets of the Nordic system, tax-financing and universalism, proved popular among the public (Jonung, 2008).

Keynesian economics dominated Nordic thinking and full employment remained the dominant public policy objective in the 1970s. An enlarged public sector helped to sustain employment and, with high taxation, provided universal services (Esping-Andersen, 1996). The perception of the Nordic states as 'strong work societies' assisted in the shift to an active labour-market approach (Kildal and Kuhnle, 2005). From there, it was a small step to what was described as a 'work approach', which incentivised participation in the labour market by linking contributions into the system with benefits. In this way, reciprocity – what you put in, you get out – began to replace universalism as an informing principle of the system.

Economic Crises

From the 1970s onwards, the 'Golden Age' of social democracy began to wane as the Nordic Model experienced several challenges. Changes in family structures, such as more single-parent families and an ageing population, were common across Europe. Some challenges, such as the increased professionalisation of the workforce, and the increase in the female workforce, were more specifically Nordic and called for changes in the welfare system. Social democrats in each of the Nordic countries identified these issues, along with the structural changes that the global economy was undergoing in the 1980s, and changed tack significantly. The public too were wary of the challenges, and political competition in the Nordic states underwent a considerable change in the 1980s and 1990s. Denmark saw 11 years of Conservative government between 1982 and 1993, with the social democrats moving to a more centrist position in order to compete. Norwegian politics was marked by a lack of left-right cooperation, a decline in support for the social democrats and weak minority governments of both sides of the spectrum. In Sweden, while the social democrats remained in government longer, they too moved rightwards amid an increase in support for their conservative rivals (Marklund and Nordlund, 1999). Changes to the welfare system were limited in nature and were not a fundamental departure from the generous provisions for which the Nordic states had become famed. Benefits in some areas were reduced, while waiting periods were introduced. Eligibility criteria for social programmes were tightened, making claiming benefits more difficult than previously. Some services in the public sector were privatised and subject to competition.

Perhaps the largest impact was felt when Keynesian economic policies were abandoned in favour of a more deregulated credit and currency market. Fluctuations in the global economy, coupled with more open and deregulated domestic economies, saw the Nordic states face substantial and lengthy economic crises. Financial deregulation led to a lending boom. Institutions financing loans for investments in commercial property fuelled substantial increases in cost and property prices increased dramatically in the period until the bubble burst. The subsequent property crash saw those same financial institutions that had financed the boom suffer crippling losses – banks and insurance companies collapsed, investments declined and unemployment rose, with the latter impacting upon each state's ability to maintain their commitment to generous welfare entitlements. However, adapting the welfare system was a secondary concern to re-establishing working economic structures, the primary objective of the respective governments in the immediate aftermath of the economic crisis.

The Danish economy suffered considerably in the immediate aftermath of the 1970s oil crisis, but during the late 1980s and into the early 1990s economic development remained relatively stable, in spite of the wider economic crisis (Kangas and Palme, 2005). After a run on the second-largest Danish bank, the central bank had to guarantee deposits in order to rebuild consumer confidence. Norway, shielded somewhat from the later crises by virtue of their oil economy, was affected from the late-1980s until the mid-1990s. However, the depth of the financial crash meant the Norwegian government was forced to nationalise almost the entire banking sector – it assumed control of the three largest Norwegian banks, and organised mergers for the smaller ones. Sweden's experience of the financial crisis only began in the 1990s, but that experience was more severe than their Nordic neighbours. The Swedish government had to provide a blanket guarantee to cover all liabilities for their commercial banks, an expensive guarantee in a time when the banks themselves saw crippling losses (Østrup, Oxelheim and Wihlborg, 2009). All three countries floated their currencies to restore competitiveness, starting with the general realignment of European currencies in 1992. The subsequent depreciation resulted in a reduction in interest rates, lower inflation and an economic recovery. Productivity and economic growth quickly improved, and negative GDP growth was quickly reversed. In Finland, GDP fell by 14 per cent between 1990 and 1993 and unemployment rose from 3 per cent in 1990 to an unprecedented 20 per cent during the 1990s. The Finnish Government devalued the Markka twice in the space of ten months (November 1991 and September 1992) and eventually, like their Nordic neighbours, decided upon floatation. Finland's geographic position on the border with the former USSR meant that trade was also disproportionately affected by the collapse of the Soviet Union. Trade between Finland and the Soviet Union/Russia fell almost overnight by 70 per cent in 1991 (Honkapohja and Koskela, 1999).

High levels of unemployment continued until the turn of the century, requiring adaptation of the Nordic model to the changed circumstances (Kiander, 2005). The key adjustment made at the time of the crisis in each case was not dramatically to alter the nature of the welfare state, but to raise tax levels while at the same time limiting public expenditure until the recovery was well under way. By doing so, the Nordic states were able to maintain their benefits at a level commensurate with their global perception as advanced social investment states (Kangas and Palme, 2005).

Adapting the Model

While dramatic changes to the welfare state were not undertaken, the social investment states in Denmark, Norway and Sweden did undergo substantial alterations in the wake of the economic crises (Stephens, 1996). A conservative government between 1982 and 1983 had already moved the political centre in Denmark rightward, with social democrats there moving from a traditional social democratic position to a more nuanced position whereby they could accept reforms to the welfare model. When they returned to government in 1993, the social democrats instituted reforms to active labour market policy in an attempt to deal with rising unemployment. They also sought to encourage Danish citizens to be more willing to take up employment when opportunities to work arose. The resultant legislation meant that unemployment benefit was to be limited to seven years, split into two phases. The first was a four-year 'passive' time, during which time employment did not need to be sought. The second was a three-year 'active' period, which gave citizens a right to assistance in job search and training and an obligation to display a willingness to find a job. A new system of active measures was introduced to provide good offers of employment to citizens without jobs (Jørgensen and Schulze, 2011). Here began Denmark's much-lauded 'flexicurity' model, combining flexibility for both employers and employees. There was some deregulation in the labour market but also security, delivered through generous, albeit strictly controlled welfare provision for the unemployed and the extension of the active labour market (Jørgensen, 2000). High unemployment through the mid-1990s meant that the system was tested vigorously in its early years.

In Norway, the lack of left-right cooperation, weak minority governments during the 1980s and 1990s and a decline in support for the social democrats meant that the Nordic model appeared weaker. The Norwegian government, like its Danish counterpart, aimed to reduce unemployment by introducing active labour market and training policies in a Solidarity Alternative agreement with unions, which reduced unit costs. In return, welfare rights, including the retention of a right to 100 per cent compensation in the event of sick leave, would be safeguarded (Dølvik, 2007). However, during the economic crisis in the early 1990s, production fell while unemployment rose to nine per cent, which placed further pressure on spending. A strong economic recovery, based predominantly on offshore investments and oil revenues saw an economic turnaround in the mid-1990s, with a general upswing in production. As unemployment came down significantly, Norway's welfare system escaped any substantive adjustments in the period.

Sweden, for so long the epitome of the Nordic Model, saw a substantial contraction of its welfare state as a result of the economic crisis of the 1990s. By the height of the crisis, the tripartite bargaining model began to erode. Tripartite bargaining had been a cornerstone of successive governments' macroeconomic policy. In particular, in helping employers' associations and trade unions come to agreements on wage increases and general business practices, as well as employment-related welfare spending, tripartite bargaining played a key role in building the trust required to maintain the generous social investment spending. Rising inflation and aggressive devaluations had, during the 1980s, meant that wages remained stagnant but the liberalisation of credit markets, low interest rates and expanding public budgets led to a steady growth and near full employment prior to 1990 (Calmfors, 1993). The tipping point came when the employers' federation SAF withdrew from wage negotiations, claiming that market-based solutions to control wages were more effective (Dølvik 2007). The end to centralised bargaining made wage restraint difficult to enforce. Swedish social democrats attempted to move towards the so-called Third Way between the Keynesian reflation policies, which had served the Nordics well to that point, and Thatcherite austerity politics. For Sweden, this meant a cut in spending as a percentage of GDP and a cut in welfare spending. It also, in 1991, saw the Swedish social democrats record their worst electoral performance since 1928 (Stephens, 1996). The incoming centre-right government attempted to deal with the crisis which by 1994 saw unemployment reach 14 per cent (Peterson, 2009) by cutting public budgets, tightening benefits, reforming public services and, increasingly, turning to private sector and managerial solutions. This was a considerable departure from the distinct Nordic model of which Esping-Andersen (1996) wrote.

Divergence in the Nordic Model

In the late 1990s, Denmark, Norway and Sweden each experienced a swift and strong recovery, with productivity and economic growth improving while unemployment returned to levels that could sustain the welfare state. Nevertheless, reforms to the Nordic welfare states during the 1990s meant considerable variation between the states. Norway, in spite of unemployment peaking at 9 per cent, was able to expand the welfare state. By 1998, the economic recovery had reduced unemployment to 4 per cent and Norway was able to lengthen maternity and paternity benefits from 35 to 52 weeks while maintaining 100 per cent replacement pay for sickness and maternity and 70 per cent replacement pay for unemployment and pensions (Eirtheim and Kuhnle, 2000). Denmark, for all the economic troubles it had faced in the late 1970s and 1980s, maintained a high level of social protection during the 1990s and the Danish welfare state remained on a similar trajectory to the Norwegian one.

By contrast, the Swedish and Finnish welfare states suffered much more as a result of the economic crisis in the 1990s. Prior to the crisis in unemployment figures in 1990 were just 1.7 per cent in Sweden and 1.4 per cent in Finland. By 1994, these figures were 8.4 per cent for Sweden and 16.7 per cent in Finland (Kangas and Palme, 2005). For a welfare state that depended upon full employment for the generous system of entitlements to function, this represented a considerable challenge. Revenues from taxation were reduced while public expenditures, notably unemployment benefits, saw a sharp increase. With the prospect of a continuing economic crisis, parties in both Sweden and Finland accepted that spending could not continue at previous levels, and thus welfare cuts would be required. Whereas Norway had maintained 100 per cent levels of replacement pay, Sweden reduced sickness, maternity and unemployment benefits from 90 per cent to 75 per cent, while Finland reduced sickness benefits from 80 per cent to 70 per cent and unemployment benefits from 70 per cent to 60 per cent and both countries increased waiting periods and tightened eligibility for benefits in an attempt to reduced public spending. Both countries also saw more widespread use of market-driven administrative practices, decentralisation of services and user-financing in some areas, a departure from the universal, tax-financing model of the 'Golden Age'.

Although it was the liberalisation of banking regulations in the 1980s that had set in motion the economic crisis, deregulation of the telecommunications sector actually assisted in the economic recovery of Finland and Sweden. Exports of high-technology increased from 8.8 per cent to 22.1 per cent of total manufacturing exports in Finland between 1990 and 2002, while in Sweden the increase was from 16 per cent to 21.9 per cent, with companies such as Nokia and Ericsson being key players (Hilson, 2008). At the same time, spending on research and development as a percentage of GDP in Finland and Sweden was highest among OECD states, while Norway and Denmark consistently ranked inside the top ten. Spending on technology thus became a feature of the Nordic states as they entered the 21st century, along with the continuation of large public sectors, and weakening, though still significant, collective bargaining systems. As a result, divergences emerged within the Nordic model. A Danish Model, with its active-labour market policy and pursuit of 'flexicurity' was lauded by the European Union as providing employees with more freedom in the labour market. A Finnish Model was developing, based on research and high-level technology exports, with an education system that was quickly making Finland a global leader in education standards. A Norwegian

Model, retaining much of the elements of the classic Nordic Model, flour-ished and expanded welfare in some areas, most notably, childcare, while Norwegian economists were ever careful not to overspend the oil fund surplus. The new Swedish Model departed from its position as flag-bearer for the Nordic Model, with a decline in corporatism and a shift in focus to macroeconomic stability, economic growth and fiscal discipline (Hilson, 2008).

A Twenty-First-Century Nordic Model?

Diversification within the Nordic Model was one consequence of the reforms required in the wake of the economic crises of the 1990s, yet the basic principles informing the model remained in place. Citizens in Nordic states remain some of the highest taxed in the world. Spending, in particular, social spending, remains high, as a means of maintaining the social invest-ment model, and universalism remains a prominent feature, although some selectivity has been introduced. The politics of deliberation, consensus and compromise remains an integral part of the system although tripartite bargaining has been weakened by declining union membership and a change in business focus.

Party politics has played a role in these changes. In Denmark's 2001 general election, a party other than the social democrats won the most seats in the *Folketinget* for the first time since 1924 and the formed first centre-right majority government since 1928 (Qvortrup, 2002). Further election victories followed in 2005 and 2007. Measures such as tighter controls on immigration – a result of the electoral breakthrough of the right-wing Danish People's Party – and a tax freeze indicated a shift from the broad consensus that had previously existed. By the time of the global financial crisis in 2008, the two issues that had brought the centre-right government to power, immigration, and a desire to see moderate reduc-tions in government spending on welfare, had been superseded by economic concerns. Unemployment rose to 7.5 per cent in 2010, which once again put pressure on welfare spending. The centre-right government's response was to reduce spending by introducing a zero-growth policy for public sector wages, while unemployment benefit was reduced further. The period of entitlement was altered again, halved from the four-year 'passive' period instituted by the reforms of the late 1990s to two years. Functionally, the welfare model in Denmark remains largely unchanged in the 21st century, but there is more of a focus on the active labour market policy and the principle of 'flexicurity', in a bid to improve not only the economic circumstances of the welfare model but also its functionality.

In Norway, the political situation in the early part of the 21st century was similar to that of Denmark. Just two months before the Danish election saw a centre-right government deal social democrats a substantive electoral defeat, Norwegian voters returned a near-identical result. Like the Danish social democrats, the Norwegian Labour Party suffered their worst electoral performance since the mid-1920s (Madeley, 2002). However, unlike in Denmark, the centre-right experience in Norway was not a prolonged one. The Norwegian Labour party returned to office in 2005, governing in a coalition with the socialist left and the centrists. Although the centre-right's period in office had been dependent on a coalition of conservative, Christian Democratic and liberal parties, with confidence-and-supply support from the right-wing Progress Party, the Norwegian economy had gone from strength to strength in this period. Unemployment remained low, aiding the government in delivering spending on social protection. Interest rates remained steady at around 2 per cent. With general economic growth during the centre-right's period in office, it took splits in the coalition, a decline in support for the prime minister and concern with government spending to bring the Labour party back into government. The centre right government's decision to utilise the oil fund surplus to fund further spending became the central issue in the election campaign (Sitter, 2005). In 2001, building on the politics of the 'Third Way', the Labour party had had to defend their own fiscal conservatism, their policy on privatisation, and the reforms in health and education that had been delivered in office in the latter years of the 1990s.

By 2005, the party had reversed these positions, arguing that the centre-right government had exceeded their mandate in this area, and that the reforms they made, including more privatisation, had weakened the Nordic model. The return to office of a centre-left coalition in 2005, and their re-election in 2009, meant that the centre-right challenges to the Nordic model that occurred in Denmark (and Sweden, discussed below) never followed in Norway. Rather, during the 2000s, Norway actually saw further expansion of its welfare state. While the global financial crisis that occurred in 2008 damaged global economies much more severely than Norway, the centre-left coalition was able to deliver a budget that provided more employment opportunities and attempted to stimulate the economy, particularly for businesses (Allern, 2009). However, in 2013, the coalition was ousted by a minority coalition government of the right, comprising the Conservative and Progress parties, the latter a right-wing populist party, with support from the smaller Christian Democrat and Liberal parties. Welfare issues played a key role in the campaign, though the focus was more on improved delivery of services and efficient administration than philosophical debate about financing welfare services.

Electoral politics in Sweden mirrored that of Denmark and Norway in 2006 with the election of the centre-right Alliance coalition heralding the end of 12 years of social democratic governments. Like their colleagues in Denmark and Norway, the Swedish social democrats suffered their worst electoral performance since 1920 (Aylott and Bolin, 2007). In truth, however, the turn away from being model student of the Nordic Model had already been made under the social democrats in the late 1990s. The election of the Alliance merely accelerated this process. In the 2006 election, the centre-right parties attacked the record of the social democrats in government, arguing that they had failed to adequately deal with rising unemployment, and that the reforms had considerably weakened the Swedish Model. The Alliance cited reductions in unemployment and sickness benefits instituted by the social democrats as evidence of the weakening of the model, but, in office, the Alliance went further. Unemployment benefits were reduced from 80 per cent to 70 per cent of salary after 200 days of unemployment, then to 65 per cent of salary from 300 days onwards. Sickness insurance was similarly affected (Aguis, 2007). At the same time, government revenue was reduced through a series of tax cuts. These included reductions in income tax for low and middle-class earners, as well as abolition of the wealth tax and streamlining of business regulation. Here, the challenge to the Nordic model was not merely functional, as the changes to the Danish system had been, but ideological. The centre-right government's reforms carried much more of an individualistic streak with less of a focus on the relationship between individual citizens and the state.

Still Social Investment States?

In spite of the changes from centre-left to centre-right governments, the Nordic states have retained their status as high-tax, high-spend states. Of the OECD countries, Denmark (60.2 per cent) and Sweden (56.6 per cent) have the two highest top marginal rates of income tax, while Finland (49 per cent) is tied for ninth and Norway (at 40 per cent) is much lower down the table. As a percentage of GDP, taxation in the Nordics has remained fairly constant. In Denmark, it has remained around 47 per cent (as a result of higher overall taxation rates) while in Finland and Norway taxation is around 42 per cent of GDP. Sweden's rate has fluctuated a little more, but it remains around 45 per cent (2010 figures, see Figure 6.1). High taxes across the four Nordic states are predominantly on labour income and on consumption (VAT), while corporation taxes, as well as capital income for individuals, remain comparatively low (Kiander, 2005). There are however, significant differences to the taxation framework in each individual state. For example, Sweden has an additional tax on property and individual wealth while individual income tax in Denmark is particularly high in order to compensate for a low level of social security contributions. Taxation at these levels also requires near-full employment in the labour market, a long-term goal of Nordic welfare states.

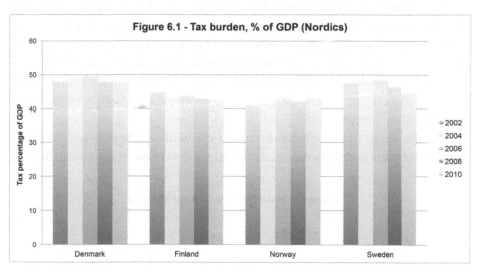

Total spending in the Nordic states (Figure 6.2) is the highest in the OECD, with Denmark, Finland and Sweden comprising three of the top four highest spending states in 2012 (with Belgium third). This is, in part, due to the principle of universalism, which ensures that the middle class is included within the benefit system. This, in turn, helps to maintain the social solidarity required to provide legitimacy to the welfare system.

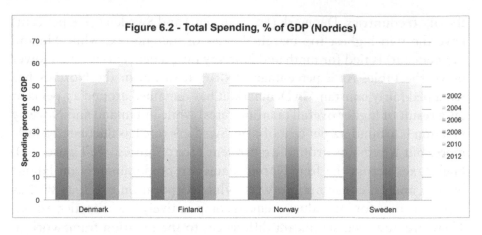

Figure 6.2 - Total Spending, % of GDP (Nordics)

The breakdown of spending suggests that Denmark, Finland, Norway and Sweden continue to spend extensively on their welfare systems. As you would expect, social expenditure, including spending on unemployment, sickness and maternity benefits, pensions, childcare and child support, among other welfare programmes, is higher as a percentage of GDP in the Nordic states than in states which pursue other models of welfare spending (Kautto, 2005). Indeed, social spending accounts for around half of all government expenditure in the Nordic states. However, despite the increased pressure on the Nordic model from the turn of the century, social expenditure levels have also remained consistent, with Denmark and Finland showing a slight increase in social spending and Norway and Sweden showing a small decline (Figure 6.3).

In the wake of the global financial crisis of 2008, neo-liberal states tended towards austerity measures to reduce government spending. Nordic

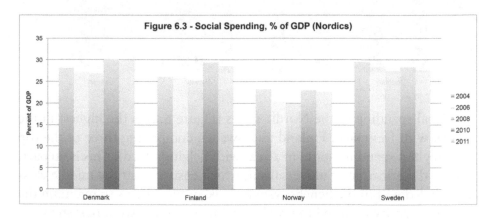

Figure 6.3 - Social Spending, % of GDP (Nordics)

states did the opposite. Social spending, which had decreased immediately prior to the crash, rose in its aftermath as each state attempted to deal with the more challenging economic environment. Attempts were made to provide more support for their citizens, particularly in the field of unemployment benefits for obvious reasons. The Nordic states had seen a rapid recovery from the 1990s financial crises which saw unemployment return to near pre-crisis levels, spearheaded by an increase in public sector employment. The global financial crisis of 2008 reversed this trend, with governments unable to afford to further expand public sector employment. As a result, unemployment rose again in the aftermath. This, once again, placed a significant strain upon the Nordic model, reducing the labour force (and with it the revenue raised from taxation on income) while increasing overall social spending on unemployment benefit.

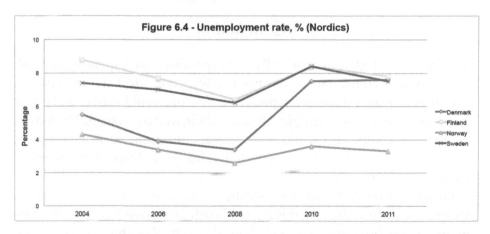

Figure 6.4 - Unemployment rate, % (Nordics)

A charge often laid against social investment states in that they lack economic sustainability and enterprise and that their large public sectors thwart any opportunity for economic growth. The economic performance of the Nordic states provides evidence to the contrary. Since the turn of the millennium, the Nordic economies have been on an upward trajectory, leaving their citizens wealthier year-on-year. GDP per capita in each state has been significantly higher since 2000. The global financial crisis had a clear impact between 2008 and 2009, with each state seeing a fall in GDP per capita and in the case of Norway, a significant fall. However, by 2011, each had recovered well, to approximately the same value as in 2008. The overall performance of Norway is of particular note. From a starting GDP per capita of $42,500 in 2004, it had risen to $61,800 by 2011 – a 45 per cent increase in a seven year period (Figure 6.5). This shows that social investment states can also allow scope for economic growth.

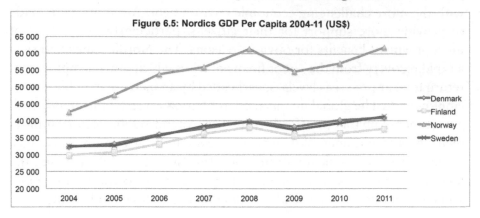

Figure 6.5: Nordics GDP Per Capita 2004-11 (US$)

Conclusion

The Nordic Model, as originally conceptualised in Esping-Andersen's typology of welfare states, comprises a Weberian ideal-typical case – a situation in which states given perfect conditions could deliver a clear set of social democratic principles through their welfare system. Of course, we live in an imperfect world, and perfect conditions never materialise, so each welfare state is a means of delivering the politics of the possible, compromising in certain areas to deliver manageable spending within the confines of revenue raised. The Nordic states are no different from other western welfare systems in this regard. Their effectiveness is governed by many factors both within and without the control of their governments. Global economic conditions, as this chapter has demonstrated, have as much, if not more, of an impact upon internal welfare systems as domestic political decisions do.

The sense of social solidarity developed during the shared experiences of the Second World War meant that the development of Nordic welfare systems in the post-war period could proceed as a universal rather than needs-based system. In the subsequent years, policy learning between the states was evident as each built a welfare system that generously supported their population. The 'Golden Age' of welfare across Europe followed, and welfare was expanded substantially in the Nordic states during this period, with Sweden leading the way. However, each state developed their welfare state at a different pace and with differing emphasises – there was no one direct path to follow in order to develop the model (Hilson, 2008). The economic crises of the 1990s affected each of the Nordic states and led to each developing different solutions in order to tackle similar problems. Denmark focused on developing the principle of 'flexicurity', and on reducing unemployment benefit in order to incentivise reintroduction into the labour market. Finland based a recovery on research and development, and a substantive telecommunications industry was the result. Norway reduced costs while maintaining wage levels in an attempt to stimulate the economy by increasing consumption. Sweden attempted to follow a 'Third Way' path between Keynesian and Thatcherite economics, a policy which resulted in significant cuts to the welfare budget. The result, in the 21st century, is a widely divergent Nordic model which continues to maintain the social democratic principles it did at its inception, notably universal and generous benefit provision, tripartite wage-bargaining processes and consensus-based institutions delivering public policy, but which has adapted to the economic circumstances of globalisation and international institutionalisation. In pursuing social investment models with distinct social democratic overtures, the Nordic states remain distinct from their European neighbours. An inability to maintain a commitment to low unemployment means that a Nordic Model of welfare continues to exist, albeit in a form which is somewhat different to that which was originally instituted. Deliberation, consensus and compromise in decision-making still exists, so too do universal benefits, albeit at reduced levels and with more complex qualifications and social solidarity, a key component of maintaining public support for the system. Maintaining a social investment state in the face of increasing economic challenges as a result of volatile global markets may, however, be the consistent factor which continues to bind the increasingly divergent component states together in the Nordic Model.

CHAPTER 7

The Baltic States. The Market Liberal Road

Transitions

UPON INDEPENDENCE FROM the Soviet Union in 1991, Estonia, Latvia and Lithuania embarked upon a rapid and radical neo-liberal trajectory, moving themselves as far from their Soviet Communist histories as quickly as they could. Rapid privatisation of formerly nationalised industries, removal of barriers to foreign direct investment, fixed currency pegs and low, flat-rate taxation were quickly introduced in all three states as a means of declaring economic independence alongside political independence. This was a double transition of simultaneous radical constitutional and economic reform (Vilpišauskas, 2014). Each was concerned that Russia remained the largest threat to their security, and that moving swiftly from a Soviet model to a western, neo-liberal model would help to solidify national independence and provide a departure from the Soviet history. In this respect, socio-economic policies and the emergence of liberal market states in the Baltics was tied specifically to nation-state building (Bohle and Greskovits, 2013). This is of note because it suggests that neo-liberal economic models were not selected necessarily for economic or normative reasons, but as part of a new identity for the independent Baltic states. Thus, some of the reasons for adopting a liberal market model such as global competitiveness, incentives for investment to encourage economic growth, and a small public sector to limit drain on productivity, were not among the primary considerations for Baltic nation-builders as they moved from centralised to deregulated economies.

Declaring Independence

The departure of the Baltic states from the former Soviet Union was an abrupt but deliberate affair. It was abrupt, in the sense that events moved hastily, and actors were also forced to make quick decisions that would have long-lasting effects. It was deliberate in the sense that the decisions made in this period were taken with a specific proviso in mind, to move the Baltic states quickly away from Soviet politics and economics. This entailed radical overhaul of the political and economic structures of the newly independent states. The double transition, as it became known, entailed considerable constitutional upheaval. The restoration of historic, imposition of temporary, and establishment of new constitutions took a considerable period of time to negotiate against a backdrop of economic turmoil, which only served to accelerate the feeling that radical economic changes were also required.

Upon independence, the Baltic economies could in no way be described as healthy. In Estonia, unemployment stood at 30 per cent and inflation rates of over 1,000 per cent were not uncommon. Trade with Russia accounted for 92 per cent of Estonian imports and exports. Industry was limited and basic food items rationed. In 1992, GDP fell by 30 per cent (Laar, 1996). In Latvia's case, prior to independence electronics and military production accounted for between 70 per cent and 80 per cent of economic output. After the collapse of the Soviet Union, the military industry fell apart overnight, with many of those in uniform quickly migrating to Russia, and electronics production moved to states with more advanced development (Rajevska, 2005). Lithuania, the first republic to declare independence in 1990, suffered political and economic sanctions, as well as military repercussions. A referendum secured the support of the Lithuanian people, but the economic situation worsened, and like Estonia, Lithuania suffered increased unemployment and rising inflation rates. For all three, the economic situation made the transition to independence a difficult task. Conversely, however, it also made the simultaneous economic transition easier to commit to since the status quo did not appear to be a viable option.

Economic Transition

Both Estonia and Latvia had to contend with large ethnic Russian populations within their borders post-independence, so that nation-building became a key consideration. The decision to proceed rapidly towards a liberal market model was, particularly in Estonia, linked to the nation-building project, and a crucial part of forming a new national identity. Latvia followed Estonia's economic lead, but the pace of change in

Lithuania was much slower. In part, there was less of a requirement for speed – Lithuania did not have the same numbers of ethnic Russians as Estonia and Latvia, and did not require the same level of nation-building, while Lithuania had been more successful in building a ruling elite in the final years of the Soviet Union than its neighbours (Bohle and Greskovits, 2013). The Lithuanian Communist Party remained largely intact, trans-forming itself into social democratic party. Although it was overtaken by a centre-right party later in the 1990s, the Communist Party ensured that there was some political discussion about the move towards a market economy. Frequent changes in leadership of political and economic institutions in Lithuania also added to the instability, and slowed the process there.

Estonia acted as a Baltic leader in the economic transition. Mart Laar, a historian-cum-politician, elected as Prime Minister in 1992 at the age of 32, famously declared that the only book about economics that he had read was Milton Friedman's *Free to Choose*. This might go some way to explaining why, in 1994, Estonia instituted a flat-rate tax of 26 per cent. Later, Laar admitted that he just thought the idea of a flat-rate tax was 'common sense' and that because he thought it had already been insti-tuted everywhere else he introduced it to Estonia. Devotion to Fried-manite economics extended to privatisation of industry, with a particular focus on foreign direct investment. This included the virtual abolition of import duties in order to encourage further inward investment and to limit the role of the state in economic policy, with exceptions in the fields of military and nuclear trade. A policy of pegging the Estonian kroon to the German Mark through a currency board meant sacrificing control over monetary policy, including interest rates. As a result, Estonia had joined Hong Kong as one of the most open economies in the world by the early 2000s (Thorhallsson and Kattell, 2012).

Much of the Latvian economic story post-independence is very similar to that of Estonia, and Estonia's leadership on economic reforms led to policy-learning on Latvia's part, including on privatisation, taxation and the currency peg. In Latvia's case, a move towards privatisation was very much a return to the pre-Soviet model, where private ownership had been encouraged. There was consensus among elites in Latvia over how to deliver a neo-liberal economic model, while the USA, in trying to extend their own influence in the formerly communist Eastern Europe, also played a role. Rapid privatisation followed, with social policy development

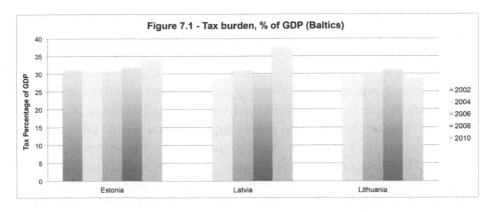

Figure 7.1 - Tax burden, % of GDP (Baltics)

downplayed. Lithuania also decided, in 1994, to introduce a currency board and peg their currency to the dollar, and later to the euro, so helping to stabilise prices. By taking monetary policy out of the hands of politicians, the currency peg was also intended to stabilise the macroeconomic environment, allowing the politicians to focus on political issues. However, much political thinking in Lithuania was geared towards the short term. Election cycles coincided with increases in spending (see Figure 7.2) in attempts to attract votes, leading to an inability to balance the budget, in marked contrast to Estonia, where a balanced budget became a constitutional requirement.

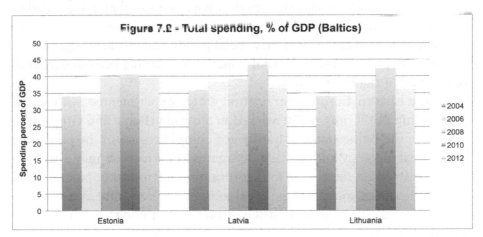

Figure 7.2 - Total spending, % of GDP (Baltics)

(No) Social Partnership

Despite a trend of declining trade union membership in much of Europe since the 1970s, trade unions continue to play a role in many western

European social and political systems. This is not the case in the Baltics. Trade union membership in Estonia and Lithuania is around 10 per cent, and a marginally higher 13 per cent in Latvia. Several key sectors, including banking, construction and small businesses, are completely union-free. In Soviet times, trade union membership was mandatory, and unions played a substantial role in redistributive activities, as well as being ideological mouthpieces for the state and providing opportunities for advancement in the Communist party. In contrast to the role of trade unions in western Europe, however, they never played a role in wage bargaining or improving workers' rights (Aidukaite, 2009) since, under the communist ideology, it was assumed that the conditions designed by the state were as good as they could be. Upon independence, trade unions in the Baltics were slow to react, and in the early period, continued to function as community organisations. The institution of liberal market ideologies meant trade unions had to develop a new role and in many industries had to be created from scratch. Membership uptake was slow, as many workers did not understand the role trade unions were supposed to play in society or see any real benefit to membership. The history of trade unions as a tool of the state rather than an organisation established to protect the interest of the workers continues to influence public attitudes towards unions in the Baltic states. The legacy of communism and the lack of any links between trade unions and political parties mean that unions tend to be weak and ineffective in negotiations, especially in Estonia (Eamets and Kallaste, 2004). The result is that social policy and workers' rights have no effective proponent, and social policy has generally been underdeveloped in all of the Baltic states.

Some eastern European transition states experimented with social partnership but it only really worked in Slovenia (Bohle and Greskovits, 2013). In the Baltic states, it hardly got going, because of the prevailing neo-liberal ideology and the lack of organised partners. It may also have been hindered by the failure to incorporate the Russian population and their consequent social and political marginalisation. One consequence was a strategy that prioritised development in the narrow sense over social cohesion.

Underdeveloped Welfare Systems

Prior to independence, the social security systems of the Baltic states were based upon a 'one-size-fits-all' policy developed for the entirety of the Soviet Union. Pensions derived from the 1956 Soviet Union Pension Act, which included only workers until 1965 and was funded solely by the state budget with no contributions from the individual. Unemployment benefit did not exist previously, since unemployment was not recognised by the Soviet government. Sickness benefits were paid by the Soviet Union for the full period of sickness, but the level of benefit was dependent upon previous work and non-union members were only entitled to half the benefit of union members. Maternity benefits were paid for 56 days before and after the birth. The Soviet Union also paid a grant to mothers for the birth of their child, doubling for second and third children and, in 1982, a year's maternity leave was provided for, with the mother receiving a flat-rate childcare allowance.

Since independence, there has been policy learning both from historical experience with the Soviet Union and from European neighbours and the European Union. In the area of pensions, substantial reforms began even prior to independence. In Estonia, separate pension schemes for workers and farmers were merged into one pot, while a new pension law was inspired by changes being made in the Soviet Union itself. One month into independence, given the financial difficulties imposed by unemployment, inflation and negative growth, the new pension law was suspended. The new state ran deficits in social spending budgets, and delays to payments were common. A brief period of flat-rate benefits saw public protests, and a further reform culminated in a new pension law adopted in April 1993. This reform included a gradual increase in the retirement age, to 65 for men and 60 for women, as well as service-related rather than earnings-related payments. A three-pillar pension system was adopted in 1997, incorporating compulsory pay-as-you-go as the primary financing element, with a mandatory state-funded tier and a private, voluntary-funded tier providing top-up funds dependent on contributions.

In Latvia, pensions were to be paid from a new Social Insurance Fund established in 1991 and funded by a new social tax, paid substantially by employers and minimally by employees. Pension payments were meant to be earnings-related but the rapidly changing economic system meant that a subsidy was needed, breaking the earnings-link, and a two-pillar system

97

was the outcome. The subsidy was subsequently replaced with a flat-rate basic pension, paid simultaneously with the earnings-related pension. However, a substantial rise in inflation in 1992 meant a further change, with the flat-rate maintained at the expense of the earnings-related pension. By 1994, and the election of a new centre-right government, pensions changed again. This time, at the recommendation of the World Bank, a three-tier system, much like Estonia's, was instituted. This combined a pay-as-you-go element with mandatory funded and voluntary private schemes. Further changes followed the 1995 election, with the introduction of a Notional Defined Contribution (NDC) system, again at the behest of the World Bank. With this new system, the annual pension paid to citizens was equal to the total of pension contributions accumulated divided by their remaining life expectancy after retirement (Müller, 2002). Several aspects influenced this reform, including the relatively low retirement age, substantial resort to early retirement distorting the ratio of workers to claimants and widespread attempts to avoid paying into the scheme. Latvia was the first state to introduce this new NDC system, and so became a testing ground for some of the principles (Cichon, 1999). However, the limited redistributive effect of NDC provided another source of tension, with large variation between the highest and lowest levels paid out in pensions, even more so after later the introduction of second and third tiers.

Upon independence, Lithuania continued to operate the Soviet pension system, though adjustments were made at several points. Reforms in 1994 introduced a two-pillar system – a contributory pension, financed through pay-as-you-go, and a non-contributory flat-rate pension, paid only to those unable to enter the labour market. In 1999, a voluntary pension scheme was also established for further contributions, but there was limited take up. Pressures for further reform were increased by the Russian economic crisis in 1998 which resulted in negative GDP growth in each of the Baltics. At the same time, defaulting on pension contributions was on the increase. The establishment of a three-pillar system, in the same mould as Estonia and Latvia, followed in 2001. A tax-financed, flat-rate pension model formed the basis of pillar one, with pillar two a specifically private pension fund. Pillar three was to remain a voluntary system, but with more provision to encourage entry into this system.

All three Baltic states established a new healthcare systems, though lengthy waiting periods and patients having to pay large sums to secure treatment were not uncommon. Twenty-first-century discussions have focused on proposals to link healthcare to taxation, but support among centre-right parties is limited. The proposal is also difficult to institute due to hidden employment and low wage levels. Wider benefits, including housing, general medical insurance and disability payments, are means-tested. Social assistance is the responsibility of the municipalities, meaning there are different levels of assistance in different areas and a race to the bottom, with municipalities keen not to be more generous for fear of migration into their region. Unemployment, sickness, maternity and child benefit are all related to earnings and designed to discourage unemployment. In Latvia, those eligible are entitled to 100 per cent of the benefit for the first three months they are claiming, 75 per cent from months 4–6 and 50 per cent for the months 7–9, based upon their earnings. Those who are nearer retirement will not be considered for 100 per cent benefit, since their working life is near complete. To be eligible for unemployment benefit a citizen requires 18 months' worth of work and contributions to the insurance scheme. As a result of limited social assistance schemes, social spending in each of the Baltics is limited (Figure 7.3).

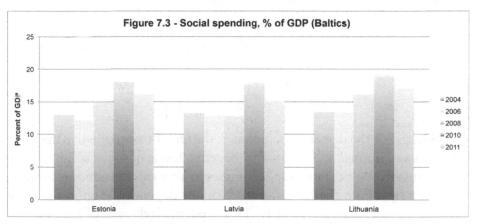

The Baltic states have experienced significant bouts of unemployment (see Figure 7.4). In contrast to the Nordic states' rather generous benefits, and active labour market policies, unemployment benefit in the Baltics is limited. Early 2000s statistics indicate that only 2 per cent of total social expenditure is channelled towards assisting the unemployed (Aidukaite, 2006). Assistance is split into two forms. Passive measures, in the form of unemployment benefits, are paid to those who are not active in the labour market. Active measures, including training and job-seeking programmes,

are targeted towards those seeking to return to the labour market. Benefits are financed through social insurance contributions from both employers
and employees. Citizenship as well as 18 months of paid employment and
social insurance contributions are required in Lithuania (with various
exceptions) while in Latvia, residency, rather than citizenship, along with
nine months of social insurance contributions is sufficient. Estonia is even
more lenient with its criteria – six months employment in the previous
year. Variations also occur in the length of time benefits are paid for, as
well as the level of benefits. Again, compared to the Nordic states, these
are relatively short periods, all less than nine months, and the level of
benefit is low. This means few even bother to claim the benefits

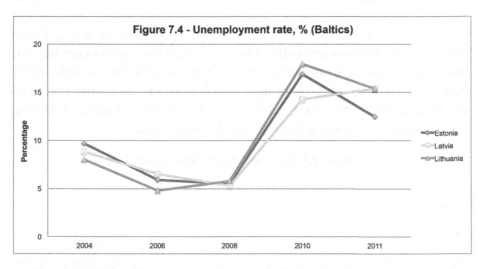

Figure 7.4 - Unemployment rate, % (Baltics)

Because of the disparity in incomes, the lack of a progressive taxation
systems and limited access to social benefits, levels of social solidarity are
low across the Baltic states. Opportunities to alter this dynamic are limited,
partially by ethnic challenges. Fifty years of dependence upon the USSR
had an impact on Baltic identity. This is particularly true of Estonia and
Latvia. At independence, 52 per cent of the population of Latvia were ethnic
Latvians, with a significant proportion of the remainder ethnic Russians.
By 2013, the corresponding figure was 60 per cent. However, in border
regions, the ethnic split is more prevalently 50–50, with some areas having
ethnic Russian majorities. In those areas, it is not uncommon for most
citizens to get their news from Russian or Belorussian television, radio or
newspapers, the latter tending to be cheaper than Latvian ones. While
citizenship immediately after independence in Estonia and Latvia was not

offered to ethnic Russians (though this changed after EU membership was confirmed) there is limited tension between ethnic communities. However, if a more generous welfare system was to be instituted, there is a perception that the ethnic Russian populations in both Estonia and Latvia would stand to benefit most from it. This is part of the reason why, politically, such a system has been seen as unattractive. There has, as a result, been a massive increase in social inequality (Bohle and Greskovits, 2013).

From Contraction to Baltic Tiger

Laar's philosophy in Estonia was to be decisive with the reforms and to take a long term view, convinced that, despite short-term pain, his reforms would be to the benefit of Estonia into the following decade and beyond (Laar, 1996). The early 1990s saw the Estonian economy suffer a substantial contraction, but the opening up of the economy meant that the public had access to many new items which had not been previously available, with oranges, other new fruits and vegetables, and car parts being particularly welcomed. Early attempts to minimise this pain by instituting a Bismarckian welfare system fell on three counts. First, it was too expensive. Second, although a public desire for a basic level of social security existed, it was tempered by the thought that the Russian part of the Estonian population would benefit the most. Third, an idea was successfully promoted that self-sufficiency and self-management were specific Estonian traits.

Strong growth from 1996 onwards led to descriptions of a 'Baltic Tiger' economy. Unemployment fell to 2 per cent, and over the following decade, the economy was one of fastest growing in the world. A collapse in Russian trade in 1998 provided a significant economic problem for Estonia, and the following three years were spent recovering from this while at the same time preparing for membership of the European Union in 2004. The latter focus, coupled with competitive tax systems for companies made all three Baltic states, but particularly Estonia, attractive for inward investment. GDP growth in Lithuania peaked in 2003 at 10.25 per cent, and in 2006 in Estonia and Latvia at 10.1 per cent and 12.23 per cent respectively. This boom was credited to the economic choices made during the transition. As a result of this, particularly in Estonia, there is little discussion of economic alternatives (Raudla and Kattel, 2011).

Bohle and Greskovits (2013), however, question Estonia's market-liberal success story. They argue that the lack of social investment has meant

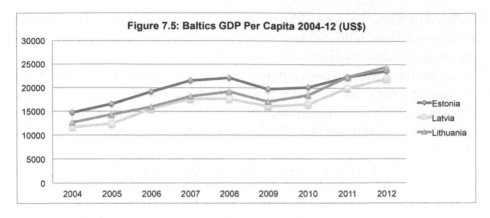

Figure 7.5: Baltics GDP Per Capita 2004-12 (US$)

a loss of the skills base and dependence on low-technology processing for re-export and Russian transit trade. The Baltic states have been less successful in attracting complex industry than the transition countries of central Europe and so remain vulnerable to low-cost competition from other parts of the world.

Europeanisation

Joining the EU in 2004, and the Eurozone later, meant that the market for Baltic produce widened considerably. Military security had been the new states' first priority after the collapse of the Soviet Union, and this meant seeking to join NATO at the earliest opportunity. However, economic security became pressing with the volatility of the Baltic economies in the 1990s and EU membership also became a priority. Opening up western markets also reduced reliance on Russia. However, open markets brought open borders and a significant brain drain. Healthcare services were particularly affected, with specialists migrating across the Baltic Sea to Finland in search of higher wages and more comprehensive social security. While doctors from Russia moved in to take their places, they lacked the qualifications necessary to become specialists, leaving a skills gap in healthcare services. Migration is also significant at the bottom level of the labour market, where Finnish rates of pay and welfare benefits are a draw for service workers.

In the 21 years from 1991–2012, the population in Latvia decreased from 2.6 million to just over two million, a consequence of negative population growth and migration, both to Russia (predominantly military families) and, post-2004, to the European Union (Rajevska, 2005). This, in turn, has had an impact on social insurance schemes and pensions. Migrants are generally of working age, leaving Latvia with a dual problem of an ageing population (tenth in the world) and a shrinking working population which, by 2012, was approximately one million people. With approximately 500,000 pensioners, this provides a ratio of workers to pensioners of 2:1. On the other hand, emigration does serve to reduce unemployment during slumps.

The story is similar in Lithuania, which has a long history of out-migration. Much Lithuanian emigration is from younger generations and the educated, who have found opportunities in the European Union. Government grappled with the problem in various ways. A Global Lithuania programme helps maintain links between families in the diaspora. Minor attempts were also made to increase the quality of services and goods available in Lithuania in order to attract emigrants to return, but there was limited success here. The official attitude was that short-term migration would help reduce unemployment and that those who left would return, bringing back with them western attitudes and experiences, but signs of this are limited.

The Crash

The global financial crisis had a massive impact on the Baltic economies. Some 97 per cent of bank balances in Estonia were held in foreign – predominantly Scandinavian – banks, which had lent excessively in the good times, contributing to economic overheating. The subsequent retrenchment in lending had a catastrophic effect on consumption and spending, while unemployment increased to 20 per cent. Public debt, hitherto very low, rose to 20 per cent of GDP.

In response, while other states were increasing borrowing in an attempt to stimulate their economies, Estonia did the opposite. Tax increases were matched by decreases in spending and salaries across the board, in some cases, by as much as 15 per cent. Legislation was introduced allowing businesses more flexibility in terminating employment, while corresponding legislation to provide assistance to those whose positions had been terminated was discussed but never implemented. It was a non-textbook response to dealing with an economic crisis. However, these measures helped to reduced Estonia's debt to around two per cent of GDP in 2009, satisfying the Maastricht criteria and allowing the country to make its long-awaited conversion to a Eurozone country in 2011. Similar responses to the crisis occurred in Latvia and Lithuania, with cuts being the primary measures taken to restore the economy. Trade union weakness facilitated these strategies. There is also wide acceptance among the Baltic populations, with governments in Estonia and Latvia returned in elections. The result was a hardening of neo-liberal philosophy and the continuation of hostility towards corporatism (Thorhallsson and Kattel, 2012). By the time of the elections, recoveries were well under way in all three states, with GDP growth returning to around six per cent by 2011.

The economic recoveries of all three Baltic states is continued evidence of their governments' emphasis on the liberal market economy, on economic prudence and, especially in Estonia, on balancing the budget. All three states suffered extensive economic damage during the crash as they had at several times during the 1990s, evidence of the volatility of liberal market states, their susceptibility to fluctuations in the global economy and their boom-and-bust cycles. The Baltics have recovered relatively quickly in comparison with southern European states like Greece, Spain and Portugal but they offer a striking contrast to their Nordic neighbours.

CHAPTER 8

Ireland. A Hybrid Case

Irish Backwardness

IRELAND IS A PARTICULARLY interesting case, since in the course of the last 30 years it has gone from being portrayed as a backward periphery, to the dynamic 'Celtic Tiger', to economic casualty. Explanations of the Irish economic miracle have been legion but they are mostly ad hoc and frequently over-determined. Everything that has happened since (usually) the mid-1980s is listed and credited with its share of success. These range from the cultural through the demographic, the institutional and the political to the more narrowly economic and external. So the Irish economic miracle is attributed to several things – popular attitudes and a culture of cooperation; the reduction of emigration and the youth of the population; corporatist bargaining and interest articulation; infrastructure investment; education; inward investment; low taxes; EU membership; and the Structural Funds. Sometimes policy-makers are given credit – more often, as befits such an eclectic list, it is attributed to luck. Ireland's subsequent troubles, however, allow us to get a more balanced picture, sorting out the positive from the negative factors.

Before independence, Ireland was economically a middle-ranking European country. Industrialisation was largely confined to the northern counties, which were to remain part of the United Kingdom. In the south, the eastern regions had long been part of a wider UK economy, with a commercial agriculture exporting to England, Scotland and Wales, while the western counties remained more marginal. This is typical of peripheral or dependent economies across the world. Economic arguments were not prominent in the nationalist movements, although in radical nationalist circles around Sinn Féin, there was a general belief that union with Great Britain had held the country back and that independence would allow a programme of national self-sufficiency.

In fact, after independence in 1922, the Irish Free State (later Republic of Ireland) continued to be dependent on the British market and remained in a currency union with the United Kingdom until 1979, when it floated its own currency within the European Exchange Rate Mechanism. After the victory in 1932 of Fianna Fail, which was to become the dominant party, the new state moved toward a policy of protectionism, inspired by visions of rural innocence. There was even a trade war with its main trading partner, the United Kingdom.

The Irish national revolution was not a social revolution. On the contrary, it actually reinforced the very social structures fostered by the British regime since the late 19th century, a conservative land-owning peasantry and a conservative, authoritarian Church. Progressive forces within the national movement were marginalised by these conservative forces and entrenched interests. The protectionist regime further rein- forced anti-modernising sectors and groups, encouraged rent-seeking and fostered a politics of distribution rather than development. Some have blamed the Catholic Church. Tom Garvin (2004: 216), in his study of why Ireland did badly for so long, claims that:

> The Republic of Ireland was unusual for many years in combining a genuinely functioning liberal democracy with most, if not all, of the standard individual rights associated with such a system on the one hand and, on the other, a popular, 'top-down' religious hierarchy which claimed a monopoly of the truth on matters of morality and many areas of public policy.

The pervasive clerical influence depended on maintaining the political and social status quo, and the control of minds. As late as 1962, 90 per cent thought that the Church was the greatest force for good in Ireland, two thirds agreed that if one followed a priest's advice one could not go wrong, and 87 per cent said that in a clash between Church and State they would back the Church.

Joseph Lee (1989) also focused on culture, identifying a lack of entre- preneurship and innovation, although he did not blame Catholicism for it, noting that other Catholic countries have done well. He did, however, detect a continued influence of the values of an agricultural society, carried over into modernity. He also, importantly, saw how traditional values did not merely survive but were constructed to form an image of an unchanging, rural and conservative society, which was actually at odds with the reality of large-scale demographic and social change.

Another pervasive feature was clientelism, often the mark of a society in transition to modernity. While clientelism and patronage politics can be traced back a long way in Ireland, they may have been reinforced by the institutions adopted after independence. The party system was defined by the divisions in the Civil War of 1922–23, which had little relevance to a modern society and discouraged new thinking. The weakness of ideological differences encourages politicians to compete in exchanging favours. The Single Transferable Vote electoral system in multi-member constituencies has the effect that TDs (members of parliament) have to compete with members of their own party to top the electoral count, and often depend on second preference votes from electors who have given their first vote to another party. So every vote counts and politics can be very constituency-focused. Politicians handle this by promising 'pork barrel' spending (money for favoured projects) in their constituencies rather than focusing on development in the broader sense.

In the absence of a vibrant civil society, it is claimed that interest groups can too easily capture public policy in favour of vested interests (Lee, 1980). Business leaders in particular can too easily catch the ear of ministers to get favours. Protectionist and agricultural interests for long held great sway over government.

So Ireland remained rural and poor, but economically dependent on Britain, which was still the main destination for its predominantly agricultural exports. Irish living standards, which were about the average for western Europe (although lower than in Great Britain) at the beginning of the 20th century had sunk to 75 per cent in 1950 and just 60 per cent by 1958 (Haughton, 2005). Massive emigration, mostly to the United States and Great Britain, kept unemployment rates down but deprived the country of many of its most dynamic young people. Such industry as developed was supported by protectionist tariffs and was not internationally competitive.

Modernisation

This all began to change from the late 1950s, when the country embarked on a programme for modernisation. Protectionism was abandoned as the emphasis shifted to competitiveness and internationalisation. The strategy can be characterised as a market liberal one, but with a key role for the state in promoting industrial development. A centrepiece of the strategy was inward investment. An Industrial Development Authority (later Agency), dating from 1949, took the lead in the 1960s in attracting overseas busi-nesses, providing a model for other countries including Scotland. There was not universal support for this policy. In the 1970s, there was a concern that foreign ownership could undermine Irish enterprise, echoed in an official report in 1981 (Lee, 1989). Similar concerns were expressed in Scotland at the same time but in both cases they disappeared as all parties promoted internationalisation.

One of the most prominent and controversial aspects of Ireland's inward investment strategy has been an emphasis on low taxes. In pursuit of investment, the government reduced corporation tax for overseas investors, a move which it had, under European rules, to extend to all firms, so that the headline rate has for some time been set at 12.5 per cent, one of the lowest in Europe. It is credited with the huge boom in inward investment, especially from American corporations. By the same token it has been criticised by other countries, notably Germany, as unfair tax competition and threatening a race to the bottom. There is also evidence that the low tax rates have attracted some 'brass plate' companies, declaring their profits in Ireland but really doing their business elsewhere.

It is difficult to know how important the low corporation tax has been in attracting investment to Ireland. The signalling effect, showing that the country is open and accommodating, might be as important as the actual financial benefits to corporations. Some observers have given more weight to the English-speaking environment, access to European markets and the young and flexible labour force. The result, however, has been the crea-tion of a very substantial and dynamic foreign-owned industrial sector and a dramatic increase in Irish living standards. The downside is that this sector is not always well integrated into the domestic economy and has not stimulated the development of a vibrant tier of Irish medium-sized enterprises. Ireland has retained elements of the dual economy, one geared to international markets and highly competitive, the other domestically oriented and less dynamic.

While Ireland did seem to be modernising and catching up during the 1960s and early 1970s, by the end of that decade it seemed to slip back again. There was a series of short-lived governments, fiscal profligacy, inflation and stagnant growth. J.J. Lee's *Ireland, 1912–1985: Politics and Society* (1989) devoted 175 pages to a pessimistic concluding chapter on 'Perspectives', diagnosing Ireland's deep-seated ills. The key elements – institutions, intelligence, character and identity – seemed deeply rooted in the national history. In retrospect, we know that this was the beginning of the Celtic Tiger and of a new turn in Irish development policy. It was also the moment at which Ireland turned to social partnership.

Social Partnership

Unlike the Nordic countries, Ireland did not have a long history of social cooperation and corporatism but the modernisation programme from the 1960s involved some effort at including social partners and reforming policy making. An Economic and Social Research Institute was founded in 1960, providing long-term policy thinking and breaking the monopoly on policy development of the conservative departments, notably the Finance Ministry. A National Industrial Economic Council was set up in 1963 and in 1973 was replaced by the wider National Economic and Social Council (NESC), including government, employers and trade unions, but it worked as a forum for discussion rather than negotiation. There had been some experiments in partnership and national bargaining in the 1970s but these had disappeared in favour of an essentially market liberal approach, with wage bargaining highly decentralised and interest groups fragmented. Given this history and the overall business culture, Ireland did not look like a promising candidate for corporatism or social partnership. Yet, in the 1980s, faced with a dire economic situation, a national consensus formed that something drastic would have to be done.

Government was looking for a way to break out of the inflationary spiral of the 1970s and set a long-term path for growth. Fianna Fail, the dominant party, was on the centre-right but had absorbed a lot of Catholic social doctrine, which emphasises class cooperation and underlies continental Christian Democracy. They also had links, although no formal affiliation, with both unions and small business. Fine Gael, the party that alternated with it in government, was less keen, being historically more pro-market, although with a social democratic wing. The Labour Party, which historically has governed in coalition with Fine Gael, has ties with the unions and was broadly in favour, although some people within it thought that social partnership might undermine electoral politics and parliament.

The business community was divided on the merits of partnership. Many business people saw advantages in simplifying wage bargaining and securing stability and predictability in wages and taxation levels. The Irish Business and Employer's Confederation signed up. As the main employers' body, they were able to present a united front, although business attitudes were by no means unanimous. American multinationals tended to stay aloof. They are hostile to trade unions and mostly refuse to recognise them, while they have a direct line into government via the America-Irish Chamber of Commerce. On the other hand, they did benefit from wage stability and predictability, which allowed them to make forward-looking investment plans. Some Irish business leaders have also been sceptical, and committed to a more liberal view of economic change.

Trade unions looked at what was happening across the water in the United Kingdom, where the Thatcher government had launched an assault on the trade unions, introduced radical neo-liberal policies and pledged to cut back the role of the state. Partnership meant compromise but this looked decidedly more attractive than the Thatcherite alternative. The weakness of the Labour Party meant that unions lacked a strong political sponsor, so they felt better off negotiating at the partnership level. Some union leaders had a wider vision, of a social democratic social investment state on Nordic lines, with bargaining extended to cover the social wage as well as conventional wage bargaining. The Irish Confederation of Trade Unions (ICTU) was a strong supporter, although it does not have a hierarchical control over its member unions, which remain rather fragmented. Some trade unions, indeed, are branches of British unions, which oppose wages policy and limits on free collective bargaining. The initial commitment to partnership was made only by a slim majority of delegates at the ICTU conference and a suspicion of partnership persisted.

The National Economic and Social Council provided the machinery for partnership, and its staff were highly influential in designing and providing the intellectual underpinning for the process. It explicitly elaborated the idea of a developmental welfare state (NESC, 2005) based on widened labour market participation. On the other hand, much of the economics profession was sceptical, wedded to the market liberal view of the economy.

Between 1987 and 2008 there were eight social partnership agreements (O'Donnell, Adshead and Thomas, 2011). The rationale was provided by a report from NESC pointing to long-term weaknesses in Irish performance and away from a focus purely on austerity. The core of the partnership was a national agreement on wages, with employers and unions at its centre. Gradually, this was extended beyond the main producer interests into broader social concerns. The Irish National Organisation for the Unemployed (INOU), founded in 1987, was brought in when the Labour Party joined government in coalition (unusually) with Fianna Fail. When the Greens entered government in 2007, environmental interests were also brought on board. Also included was the Conference of Religious of Ireland, formed in 1983. The trade unions and employers tended to resist this expansion and, as they would see it, dilution of social partnership, so they were included in a separate Community and Voluntary Pillar, consisting of 'rooms' meeting separately. The National Economic and Social Forum was established in 1993, bringing in a range of voluntary groups. While extending the representativeness of social partnership, however, the inclusion of the voluntary sector may have weakened its effectiveness since, unlike unions and employers, these groups had little to bring to the table apart from a general sense of legitimating the process by making it less exclusive. Tensions between the narrow wage-based core of the arrangement and the broader social agenda persisted.

There were also efforts to deepen social partnership at the local and sectoral level. A range of bodies was created to manage industrial relations and improve workplace conditions. Local partnerships were established under the aegis of the European Structural Funds. The idea was to spread the culture and practice of partnership beyond the core bargain.

Europeanisation

Europe provided another force for change. Ireland joined the (then) European Economic Community along with the United Kingdom in 1973. It had little choice, given the dependence on British markets and there was concern about whether Irish products could compete in the wider market. As it happened, Ireland adapted well to Europe. It was a major recipient of Structural Funds as these expanded after 1988, benefiting as well from the Common Agricultural Policy. By 1991, these transfers accounted for as much as 6.5 per cent of Irish GDP (Haughton, 2005). European markets have allowed Ireland to diversify away from dependence on the United Kingdom and it has even been said that it was only on joining Europe that Ireland really became independent of Britain. Access to Europe has also helped attract American investment. Irish governments have taken European engagement seriously, proving effective negotiators and networkers, and are recognised as one of the more effective small states in working the system. Ireland's decision to join the Euro in the first round represented a huge commitment to the European project and a decisive break with the British connection, given the UK decision to remain outside. It was criticised at the time by many economists, who believed that Ireland could not sustain the necessary fiscal and wage discipline to remain competitive. For the political class, however, Euro membership was evidence that Ireland had come of age as European state and economy.

Yet the Irish have had an ambivalent relationship with Europe. While substantial funds were flowing into the country, there was a broad consensus that Europe was a good thing. Yet national sovereignty remains a sensitive issue. The country has not been as thoroughly Europeanised as some of the older continental member states and there have always been political forces ready to use Europe as an opportunity to play the nationalist card. Following a ruling by the Supreme Court, the Irish constitution requires a referendum on membership and treaty changes and these have been marked by populist movements challenging the elite consensus. Voters have rejected two of the nine changes proposed to them (the Nice Treaty in 2001 and the Lisbon Treaty in 2008), amid campaigns that displayed very low levels of knowledge of the issues. For example, campaigners against the Lisbon Treaty alleged that it would lead to Irish citizens being conscripted into a European army. Ireland's negative vote could have killed off the Lisbon Treaty, which itself had replaced the European constitutional treaty voted down in France and the Netherlands. Because it is a small state, however, it was not allowed to do this. Instead, it was invited to vote again on both occasions, accepting the changes the second time around. The same thing happened to Denmark in 1992 after it had rejected the Maastricht Treaty.

The Celtic Tiger

The period of social partnership and the European single market coincided with a spectacular growth of up to ten per cent a year in the Irish economy. From being one of the poorest countries in western Europe, it became one of the richest. Just as a range of explanations were deployed to explain its failure in the 1950s, so observers had some apparently easy explanations for success. For some, it was low corporation tax, but exporters had already enjoyed low taxes in the 1960s. Others emphasised European funds, but these had flowed in massively after Ireland joined the European Community in 1973, without sparking off a virtuous cycle of development – in fact they seem rather to have encouraged speculation and property inflation. Many observers credited an expansion in education from the 1960s but this had merely brought Ireland up to European standards. Social partnership was cited by some. Many people cited demographics, emphasising the young population, but in the past this had merely led to emigration and the loss of many of the brightest talents.

A plausible explanation is that Ireland was experiencing the catch-up that less developed economies can enjoy when they enter into free trade with more advanced ones. In this view, it was not the boom that needed explanation, but the retarded development that preceded it. That might explain why Ireland caught up with the United Kingdom – it would not, however, explain why it overtook it.

The subsequent spectacular crash of the Irish economy allows us to address this question more easily. The economic advances of the 1990s represented a move into industry for the first time, especially in the electronics sector, where Ireland provided a good platform for conquering European markets. Its very lack of an established heavy industrial structure may have facilitated the adaptation to a modern, high technology age. The Celtic Tiger metaphor, however, concealed important weaknesses, and the expansion beyond the catch-up phase was based on an unsustainable bubble.

Ireland decided to be in the first wave of countries to join the Euro on its launch in 2000. This was essentially a political decision, seen by the political class as a sign of its economic maturity and final independence from Britain. Most economists, on the other hand, were sceptical. Ireland had only established its monetary independence in 1979 with the decision to delink the Irish pound from Sterling and there were concerns about imposing a new hard currency constraint and about its ability to compete within the Euro straitjacket. Euro membership brought low interest rates, which provided a boost for growth but were the opposite of what a booming economy needed.

Given the inability to raise interest rates, governments should have tightened fiscal policy by raising taxes and restraining expenditure so as to generate a budget surplus and contain demand. Successive Irish governments were not strong or bold enough to do this. Instead, low interest rates sparked off a speculative property boom (as they did in Spain at the same time). The close relationships of property developers with politicians, especially in Fianna Fail, protected them and allowed development to get out of control. There was also widespread corruption. As so often happens, corruption was known about for a long time but, as long as the good times lasted, it was not tackled head on. For example, it was only after his death that the affairs of the long-serving Prime Minister Charles Haughey came to light, although the manifest discrepancy between his ostentatious wealth and his official income had been there to see all along.

During the 1990s and early 2000s, Ireland, like Iceland and the United Kingdom, had encouraged the rapid expansion of banking and financial services. The sector was allowed to grow too fast and too irresponsibly, with little effective control. Large banks were encouraged out of all proportion to the size of the country, enjoying an implicit government guarantee against default. Again, the problem was exacerbated by the banks' close connections with the political class.

It is a reflection on the weakness of Irish institutions that nobody was able to call a halt to the boom in time. Politicians were able to put off difficult decisions and there was no real counterweight to the political class. Instead, politicians, advisors and the social partners tended to a form of groupthink or wishful thinking. While anyone could rationally see that in the long run the boom was unsustainable, nobody had an interest in acting on this knowledge as long as they could extract their share while it continued. Of course, this also happened in the United Kingdom around the same time.

Social partnership delivered wage stability and tamed inflation and did play a positive role in Ireland's adaptation. On the other hand, it never quite developed into a fully-fledged model of concertation or corporatism. It was undermined by the small reach of trade unions, who cover only about a third of workers, down from almost half in 1990 (Dellepiane and Hardiman, 2012). So, compared with the Nordic countries, trade unions still represented a partial and not a general interest. More effort was invested in protecting individual incomes rather than the social wage in the form of public services and long-term social investment. There were certainly increases in spending on infrastructure, education and health, but these did not match the growth of the economy as a whole. As social partnership developed, public sector workers, who are quite highly union-ised, benefited disproportionately. A 'benchmarking' exercise was aimed at addressing relativities but this proved particularly expensive as it led to spiralling claims and concessions.

Although Irish public spending did increase markedly during the boom, as a proportion of GDP it remained well below Nordic levels until the economic crash caused it to explode (Figure 8.1). The taxation system remained inefficient and government revenues were over-dependent on the boom in property and financial services. Overall taxes never reached the Nordic levels needed to underpin the social investment model (Figure 8.2).

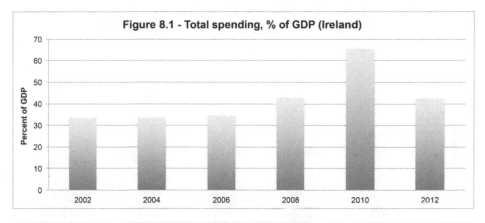

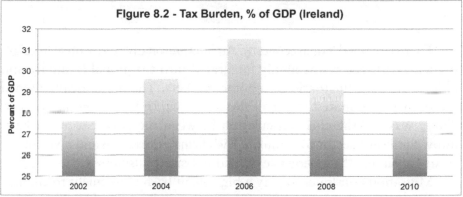

The social effects of the Celtic Tiger have proved controversial. Radical critics argue that social partnership gave the unions nothing, merely demobilised them in the interests of multinational capital, while co-opting social welfare groups (Kirby and Murphy, 2011). Defenders of the practice point to the alternatives as being a great deal worse and to the usefulness of partnership in social learning. Living standards for most people rose. Poverty declined as a result of rising employment but social inequality remained one of the highest in Europe (Dellepiane and Hardiman, 2012). Welfare payments did increase and generally remain above those in the UK, but social spending never reached Nordic levels until the economic crash led to an explosion in emergency support (Figure 8.3). So, while there was considerable investment in social and public services during the boom, Ireland never really became a social investment state. The developmental aspects of welfare and labour market policy were poorly elaborated and unable to set long-term trends and expectations.

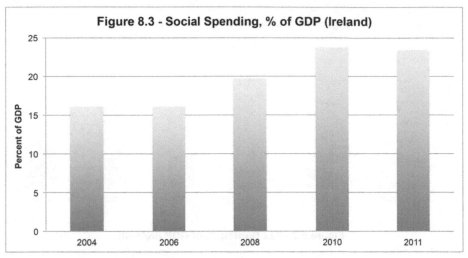

There remained a dual economy. An internationally competitive, foreign-owned (FDI) sector was highly integrated into the global economy and able to ride out fluctuations in home markets. The domestically-owned sector was dominated by small firms producing for the home market. There was not the close articulation between the two that might have allowed the FDI sector to stimulate Irish firms or research and investment, or to encourage the emergence of medium-sized businesses.

Migration continues to play a big role in Irish adjustment to change, even as Irish commentators were rejoicing at the end of the migration culture during the Celtic Tiger phase. The boom was in fact helped not just by the end of emigration but also by a surge of immigration. After the crash, emigration resumed, both of Irish people and of the incomers, many returning to central and eastern Europe. As a result, Ireland had by far Europe's biggest rate of net immigration in 2006 (22 per thousand population) and the biggest rate of net emigration in 2012 (seven per thousand) (Eurostat data).

While Ireland was committed to the European project, its model of capitalism remained that of the Anglo-American liberal market world rather than the coordinated capitalism of the traditionally more corpora-tist countries. This limited the scope of social partnership and negotiation. As the boom continued, there developed a certain hubris about market liberal mode of development, which led to a neglect of the longer term problems that were accumulating. The feeling developed among some circles that Ireland was part of global capitalism and could do without Europe and its associated social model. Ireland, in the expression of the time, moved 'nearer to Boston than Berlin', an image that covered every-thing from modes of capitalism to taxation, identities and welfare provision.

The Crash

The Celtic Tiger phase came to an abrupt halt in the global economic crisis of 2008. The immediate cause was the collapse of the over-extended Irish banks and a rash decision by the government to guarantee them completely. This overwhelmed the Irish economy and wrecked the public finances, requiring a bailout from the European Union. The decision to guarantee the banks was widely criticised but the longer-term mistake was to allow them to become so big in the first place. Like Iceland, Ireland was exposed as a small state playing out of its league since, while similarly bad decisions were made in the United Kingdom, it was more easily able to bear the consequences. Before the crash, Irish public finances had looked reasonably healthy but, again like the UK, the tax base was excessively reliant on financial services and property transactions, so that it collapsed rapidly. There followed several years of massive austerity and cutbacks in public spending. The steady growth of the economy was put into sudden reverse and unemployment climbed sharply, in spite of the reduction in the labour force from migration. It was only in 2014 that Ireland officially emerged from the bailout (Figure 8.4).

Social partnership was another victim of the crash. A proposed new agreement was abandoned and there have been no new ones since. Instead of being negotiated, austerity was imposed by government, with the Ministry of Finance regaining its ascendancy and marginalising the pro-growth and developmentalist parts of government. Critics of social partnership from the market liberal perspective claimed vindication as partnership was bundled up with the other mistakes made in the boom years. There are some continuing elements of social dialogue and the culture of partnership,

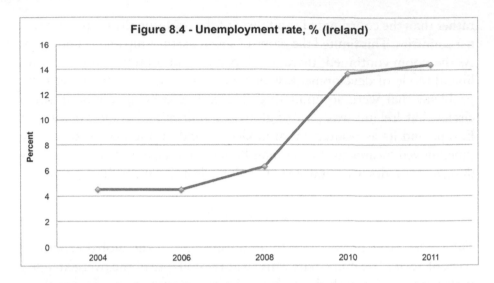

Figure 8.4 - Unemployment rate, % (Ireland)

as opposed to the practice, is still there. This could explain the relatively muted response to the crisis compared with southern European countries, where opposition has taken to the streets but the old institutions, notably the political parties themselves, have been seriously weakened so that it is difficult to see where a new effort at partnership could begin.

Ireland must be seen as a hybrid case, an effort to graft a social investment and partnership model onto an essentially market liberal structure in an effort to have the best of both worlds. The deeper institutional changes needed to underpin social investment were not carried through. Ireland has modernised rapidly and is still among Europe's wealthier

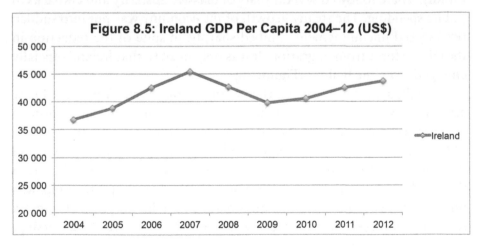

Figure 8.5: Ireland GDP Per Capita 2004–12 (US$)

countries, even following the dip from 2007 (Figure 8.5). The foreign direct investment sector, tied into global markets, came through the crash rather well. Ireland is not, however, to be compared with the Nordic states as an example of the 'high road' to development.

CHAPTER 9

How Does Scotland Compare?

The Choice of Roads

SMALL STATES CAN survive well in a globalised world and in the European single market, but there are serious choices to be made about the best route to follow. We have sketched out two ideal types, the liberal market state and the social investment state. The Baltic states have generally followed the former road and the Nordic countries, in all their variations, have chosen the social investment model. The Nordics added a social democratic dimension to maintain a high degree of social cohesion, although this has come under increasing pressure. Ireland sought to combine the models and, while it did experience impressive growth, it never became a real social investment state and remains a country of great social and economic inequalities. It is not therefore possible to mix and match elements of the two models, as each has its own logic and choices in one area, such as taxes, have implications in other fields, such as social and welfare policy.

There have been advocates of the liberal market strategy in Scotland. While out of parliament, Mike Russell (later SNP Cabinet Secretary for Education) and Dennis MacLeod wrote a book promising exactly that, with a drastic reduction in the role and size of the state and of public spending and taxes (MacLeod and Russell, 2006). This was widely seen as an effort to out-Thatcher Margaret Thatcher and seems to have riled the SNP leadership sufficiently for them to have had the text toned down between proof and publication (Macwhirter, 2006). The original must have been explosive stuff indeed. Russell later seems to have repented after entering office in a predominantly social democratic SNP government (Gardham, 2012) but the option has been canvassed by right-of-centre think tanks such as Michael Fry's Wealthy Nation (www.wealthynation. org) and some former Conservative politicians (Monteith, 2012). Conservatives have suggested that they may use tax discretion to lower rates, but no mainstream political party is currently committed to drastic retrenchment. This is not to say that this could not be a serious option in the future for a reconstituted political right in Scotland.

To date, however, no mature welfare state, with the exception of New Zealand in the 1980s has succeeded in rolling back the state to the required degree, not even the UK of Margaret Thatcher. The Baltic states are another matter, since they were undergoing a threefold transition, to independence, democracy and a market economy and the tolerance of the population to harsh treatment was rather high. Even were a Scottish Government inclined to undertake such shock therapy, the resistance of organised groups and the electoral penalty would surely deter them. In fact, the pro-independence campaign in Scotland increasingly emphasised the defence of welfare in the face of neo-liberal policies coming from the south. The SNP still contains both market liberal and social democratic elements but its oft-stated aspiration is to imitate the Nordic states. The Jimmy Reid Foundation's (2013) Common Weal, the Scottish Council of Voluntary Organisations (SCVO, 2012) and the Scottish Trades Union Congress (STUC, 2013) have all supported variants of the social investment model, with or without linking it to independence. The late Stephen Maxwell (2013, 2014) eloquently made the case for an independent social democratic Scotland. The first question to ask is therefore whether Scotland has the preconditions for such a strategy, given its starting point within the United Kingdom.

Where Stands Scotland Now?

An independent Scotland, with about five million people, would be a small European state comparable with the Nordic countries. Indeed those countries are a constant point of reference in the debate. The Scottish Government's performance framework refers frequently to other small countries as its base of comparison. The independence White Paper is replete with mentions of small states. It is now generally accepted that Scotland could survive as an independent country. Indeed most of its weaknesses are the same as those of the United Kingdom as whole, which might cause unionists to pause for thought.

Scotland's social structure resembles that of the UK and has tended to converge over recent decades, even as political behaviour has diverged (McCrone, 2001; Paterson, Bechhofer and McCrone, 2004). Scotland has experienced deindustrialisation and its economy has become dangerously dependent on consumer spending and an inflated housing market, which gives people the illusion of wealth and encourages them to borrow. The financial sector has over-expanded at the expense of the productive economy, creating vulnerabilities exposed in the financial crisis of 2008. So Scotland would not start in the place it might like to be.

Much of the debate on independence focused on public finances and the ability of Scotland to afford a generous welfare state and public services. This was a sensitive matter for unionists, who wanted to suggest that Scotland would have difficulty paying its way but know that this could look like accusing the Scots of not being able to look after themselves. It might have also undermined their case to suggest that 300 years of union had left Scotland's economy unable to generate sufficient revenues to support its needs. Compared with other cases of secession or potential secession, the economic differences between Scotland and the rest of the United Kingdom are, in fact, rather small. In recent years, Scottish GDP per capita has been around 96 per cent of the UK average. The fiscal balance has also been in equilibrium, with Scottish contributions to the Treasury corresponding to its receipts and the notional deficit of an independent Scotland being no worse, and usually slightly better, than that of the UK. This, however, is highly dependent on oil revenues, without which Scotland would be in a much worse fiscal position than the remaining UK (rUK). The problem is not in taking these revenues into account, as they are part of Scottish wealth, but rather in their volatile nature and their disproportionate weight in a small economy, with the dramatic changes in oil price in the early part of 2015 evidence of that volatility. The SNP, by calculating oil receipts back to the 1980s, argued that Scotland should be debt-free, having paid so much more than it has received. Unionists, looking at projected oil revenues in the future, argued that Scotland would be in trouble.

Nationalists argue that an independent Scotland could manage its oil resources better than the UK has done – many people agree that they could hardly do worse. The SNP proposed an oil fund, with two purposes: to balance revenues over the medium term and even out fluctuations; and to provide a long-term endowment on the lines of Norway's sovereign wealth fund and so ensure that oil leaves a legacy. It is widely accepted nowadays that the UK made a mistake in not establishing an oil fund in the past (McCrone, 2013) although none of the UK parties is currently proposing to remedy this. The problem for the SNP lay in the situation they would inherit in 2016, of a still considerable budget deficit. If oil revenues were to be invested in endowment and stabilisation funds, they would not be available to bridge the immediate deficit.

Inequality grew rapidly during the 1980s, along with that in the rest of the United Kingdom and at present are about the UK average, if London is taken out – levels in London are quite massive (Bell and Eiser, 2014). In international comparisons, Scotland is a very unequal society and, although the Nordic countries have experienced rising inequalities in recent years, they are still considerably more egalitarian than Scotland and the rest of the United Kingdom. This gives them a head start on an independent Scotland in pursuing a social democratic strategy.

A Social Democratic Scotland?

It is often assumed that Scotland is naturally a more egalitarian society than England. This stems from national traditions and myths such as the 'lad o' pairts', who can rise according his (or her) own talents, and from the wider access to education in Scotland at least until the mid-twentieth century. Apart from some years in the mid-20th century, progressive parties have usually won elections even when Conservatives were triumphant in the south. Examination of public attitudes through opinion surveys, however, shows a less clear picture (Rosie and Bond, 2007; Curtice and Ormiston, 2011). Scottish voters tend to be slightly to the left of those in England on matters such as the role of government, redistribution and attitudes to the poor. The differences are not, however, big enough on their own to underpin a radically different policy trajectory. In the 1980s and 1990s, part of the difference was explained by the fact that voters in England were not as far to the right as was often assumed – the English were not convinced Thatcherites. Rosie and Bond (2007) suggest, moreover, that the main difference was not between Scotland and England but between the south of England and everywhere else. Scottishness was, however, used as a vehicle to express opposition to Thatcherism in a way that was not available in England. Scotland was thus discursively reconstructed as a haven of social democracy. Attitudes seem to be related to economic conditions, so that in the early twentieth century, both Scotland and England moved to the right, while since the recession both have moved back somewhat to the left (Curtice, 2013).

This might suggest that Scotland is not particularly fertile territory for social democracy. Yet public policies do not emerge directly from unmediated public opinion. They are the result of the search for common ground among competing interests, from social and political compromises and from party competition. As individuals, people may not like paying taxes, supporting the unemployed or redistributing to the poor, but accept that these are the price for maintaining social cohesion and, indeed, economic growth. They can only do this, however, if there is an institutional framework within which such positive-sum social compromises can be struck. Since the 1980s, party politics in Scotland has increasingly been dominated by two social democratic parties (Labour and the SNP), whose policies on the main economic and social issues are rather similar, while their positions on the constitution have become the main line of division between them. The middle classes are more likely to vote for left of centre parties than they are in England. In England, on the other hand, the main electoral battlegrounds are the marginal seats in the south, pushing competition to the right.

There may also be a greater acceptance of government and public-sector provision in Scotland. Again, differences among the general public are rather small, since voters everywhere tend to be unenthusiastic about the introduction of private provision into health and education (Curtice and Heath, 2009). The one persistent difference is that Scots have not given up on comprehensive education as have people in England. Yet efforts by Conservative governments during the 1980s and 1990s to introduce market principles to the Scottish public services largely failed, not because they were not legislated for but because they were not taken up. Professional groups also seem more inclined to public provision and equality (Keating, 2010). Successive Labour/Liberal Democrat and SNP governments in Scotland have shown a greater respect for public service than Conservative or New Labour governments in England and much less obsession with competition as the sole principle for assuring good provision.

The Independence Prospectus

The Scottish Government's (2013) White Paper on independence was clearly inspired by the social investment perspective, with strong social democratic undertones. There were references to the experience of small, independent countries and the way that they have been able to focus their efforts. Competitiveness was central to the argument and there was an emphasis on science, research and development, human capital and infrastructure. Growth and social cohesion were not presented as alternatives but rather as complementary objectives. Skills, high levels of trust and reductions in inequality were presented as contributions to growth as well as social cohesion.

This is all consistent with a social investment strategy and a social democratic tilt to policy. Yet it coexisted within the White Paper and SNP strategy generally with a market liberal approach focused on low corporate and personal taxation. It was proposed to cut corporation tax to three percentage points below whatever level is chosen in the rest of the United Kingdom. We have already cast doubt on the efficacy of such tax competition in a mature economy and, whatever its long-term effects, it would result in an immediate fall in revenues. Neighbouring jurisdictions, including the remaining United Kingdom, would not take kindly to this behaviour and this would reduce their willingness to cooperate on other common interests. The White Paper also proposed to cut, and eventually abolish, Air Passenger Duty in an effort to attract more air traffic. This won plaudits from the heads of British Airways and Ryanair but sits uneasily with a commitment to social equality. It also makes much more difficult pledges about reducing pollution and tackling climate change.

There was a proposal in the White Paper to roll out universal childcare. Again, we were told that this would pay for itself, since it would enable more women to go out to work, so increasing the labour force and thus helping growth. It is true that childcare features in most social investment strategies as a policy with positive social as well as economic effects but that is as part of a broader set of policies about labour markets and growth. Simply introducing more childcare without more well paid jobs for women to take is not going to produce growth. On taxation as a whole, the White Paper was largely silent, apart from a pledge that rates will not get out of line with those in the rest of the UK.

There was a lot of debate on the SNP's proposal for a monetary union allowing it to continue using the Pound sterling. This would enormously constrain Scotland's capacity for macroeconomic management as monetary policy, including interest rates, would continue to be set by the Bank of England (Armstrong and Ebell, 2013). SNP policy is to claim a share of ownership and management of the Bank of England, so ensuring that Scottish interests are taken into account but, whatever arrangement was negotiated, Scotland would still be the junior partner and the Bank, which has operational independence, would not necessarily take it into account.

Monetary union would also, as the SNP accepted, entail some sort of fiscal pact such as exists in the Eurozone, further constraining Scottish policy choices. The UK Government has now made it clear that such a partnership, including joint ownership and management of the Bank of England would not be on offer. Scotland could still continue to use the Pound as its currency in various ways, but this would mean no say whatever over monetary policy.

An independent Scotland without its own currency would not be entirely bereft of economic instruments but, unable to use monetary policy including interest rates, would rely more on fiscal policies, including taxes and spending, for economic stabilisation. An oil fund would be even more essential in order to even out economic fluctuations, which of course means that the revenues could not also be used to plug the immediate spending gap after independence. The result, again, is that Scotland could be a higher tax country.

The SNP have been criticised for wanting Nordic-style public services with British levels of taxation and the White Paper did not still these criticisms. Social democratic social investment states have, as we have seen, higher levels of taxation. This is not merely a matter of taxing the rich, since in Scotland there are not enough of them and they do tend to be rather mobile (Bell and Eiser, 2014). The Nordic countries, rather, have broad tax bases, which are matched by universal public services. Value added taxes are important here. Another potential source of revenue, backed by economists of both right and left, is taxation of land and property. Such taxation is difficult to avoid, it is largely progressive and it can enhance economic efficiency by discouraging land hoarding and sub-optimal uses. It may also serve to dampen property inflation. Yet domestic rates in Scotland have been frozen since 2007 and no political party appears ready to embrace the issue. The Common Weal project sponsored by the Jimmy Reid Foundation does face up to this issue but even they seem to shy away from taxing the middle classes as a way of providing universal benefits.

Taxation is part of the social investment package but such is the level of inequality in Scotland that redistributive taxation alone cannot redress it (Bell and Eiser, 2014). There are stark inequalities in both wealth, built up over generations, and income. More egalitarian countries contain inequality by taxation but also by having a less steep gradient of wages in the first place. This an idea which Labour leader Ed Miliband caught on to at one point, although he rather lost his audience by calling it 'predistribution'. Labour failed to grasp that the secret to getting a more even spread of wages is to extend collective bargaining and enhance the rights of trade unions. As we have seen, trade union membership in the Nordic countries, while falling, is still higher than in Scotland. National wage bargaining and social pacts can also help to reduce inequalities and sustain the 'social wage' as well as individual real wages. To get there, Scotland would need to reform its institutions and ways of making public policy, as well as rethinking social partnership.

Successive Scottish governments have struck a distinct note on migration from their counterparts in London, welcoming incomers as a necessary part of the labour force, improving skills and providing wage earners to support an ageing population. In fact, under the Labour Government, immigration did increase markedly and the UK was one of the countries to open its labour markets immediately to workers from the new EU member states in 2004. Political rhetoric in England, however, remained rather hostile to immigration and by the end of the first decade of the 2000s had turned quite toxic. In Scotland the issue has been so framed that pro-immigration stances do not appear to attract a political penalty. This does put Scotland in an advantageous position with regard to attracting needed workers, although it is not clear that the numbers will be sufficient to fill the gap. At its height in the 2000s, net immigration into the UK was less than five per 1,000 of the population, compared with 22 in Ireland and 17 in Spain. The White Paper proposed a points system to meet skills shortages and more generous treatment for students, rather than a general relaxation of immigration controls.

Government

Scotland is a small country in which the key actors in many fields of public life know each other personally and lines of communication are short. There are overlapping networks in central and local government, the professions, business and civil society. There is a broad consensus on the main lines of policy, which should facilitate working together. Yet in many ways it is still organised as a 'regional' part of a wider UK political system, rather than a self-governing nation, able to mark out its own policy trajectory.

At the moment of devolution in 1999, the Scottish Government (then called Scottish Executive) inherited the apparatus of the old Scottish Office, which had grown gradually over a hundred years to manage most domestic policy in Scotland, with the big exceptions of taxation and social security. The Scottish Office was not, however, a policy-making body and indeed its capacity to make policy had actually declined during the years of Conservative government, when its job was to apply policies decided elsewhere. It was organised like a Whitehall ministry, on traditional functional lines, and divided into departments. These might have been a bit better connected than their counterparts in London but there was a weak capacity to think across government as a whole. The Scottish Office itself had the task of tweaking policy to Scottish conditions but was above all a lobby, seeking to defend Scottish interests at the centre and ensure a northward flow of resources. Adapting to becoming a government in itself took quite a long time, especially as under Labour there was still a tendency to look to London so as not to embarrass the party at the centre. Initiatives like the adoption of a distinct system of care for the elderly under Henry McLeish could provoke a serious reaction from UK Labour.

Over time, the Scottish Government has reformed to suit the circumstances of a multifunctional administration of a small country (Keating, 2010). Departments were abolished and the government reorganised on the basis of directorates corresponding to policy tasks. Hierarchies were flattened and ministers have more direct links with civil servants working on policy proposals, even at relatively junior levels. There is a National Performance Framework, which is intended to allow proposals to be appraised in relation to broad policy objectives and to assess performance in meeting them. This is the kind of reform that is possible in a small system, which would be more difficult in a large administration.

On the other hand, the budgetary process is not clearly linked to priorities or the performance framework. As a spending department that did not raise revenue, the old Scottish Office had limited discretion in allocating money between priorities and was generally concerned to maximise the amount it could get from the centre. This was determined by the famous Barnett Formula, which gives Scotland a population-based share of whatever increase or cut is being applied to comparable English programmes – but there has always been an element of discretion so that the actual outcome is a result of political compromise. For the lack of an agreed alternative, Barnett was simply rolled over into the devolution settlement. This does not encourage ministers to think about the balance between taxation and expenditure. The Scottish Government does not have to follow the English priorities that generate the Barnett consequentials and can apply its block grant at will, but there are political pressures to match what is happening down south. For example, the Scottish Government followed its UK counterpart in promising to protect health spending from the current austerity cuts.

What is lacking is a central capacity within the Scottish Government to set priorities and allocate spending accordingly. In Whitehall, it is the Treasury that plays this role and, over recent decades, its dominance has increased, extending its reach into vast areas of domestic policy, especially under Gordon Brown. Such a centralised system is neither necessary nor desirable in a small country, where it would risk stifling initiative. A smaller and more collegial mechanism for determining priorities would be better.

Policy innovation in Scotland has been inhibited by the dearth of policy institutes and think tanks such as are found in other national capitals. This is partly a matter of scale, since small places do not have the depth of resources and people that larger nations can command. This makes it all the more important to deploy such resources as exist. One of these is the civil service, which since the 1980s has been seen as an agent for delivery rather than policy ideas. Other small nations, such as New Zealand allow their public servants more scope to develop ideas and air them in public. Similarly, in local government, the health services and other public agencies, there is a potential capacity of new ideas. Indeed, back in the 1960s and 1970s, these were arguably more innovative and bold than they subsequently became.

There was much talk at the time of devolution of a 'new politics' in which the Parliament would have a central role. There would be less partisanship and a more consensual style. Committees would play a stronger role both in the legislative process and in holding ministers to account. The Parliament has certainly become the centre of political life in Scotland, it is quite accessible and polls show that is trusted more than Westminster. On the other hand, it is essentially a Westminster-style institution. Party discipline is, if anything, stricter than at Westminster and there have been few independently-minded MSPs. The committees have failed to develop real expertise in their fields or to become important actors in the policy process. Indeed, Westminster committees, especially where they have a strong and independently-minded chair, have increased their weight and even have overtaken their Holyrood counterparts.

Policy Communities

Over the last hundred years, Scotland has lost much of its indigenous business, especially the medium-sized firms that in other countries have fostered innovation and provided dynamism for the wider economy. The tendency, as elsewhere in the United Kingdom, is for small businesses to expand to a certain size and then sell out to a larger firm. The lack of indigenous ownership was seen as a problem in the 1970s and 1980s, but concern subsequently abated in the rush to attract foreign direct investment. The weakness of what the Germans call the *Mittelstand* is not only an economic problem – it also underlies the weak commitment to social partnership and to a Scottish business perspective.

Representative groups in Scotland have long been divided between those that operate only in Scotland and those that are branches of UK-wide groups. Among the former are groups in areas that have long been regulated and administered separately in Scotland, like the law and education. In these fields, distinct policy communities operated, including professional groups, trade unions, civil servants and politicians. Policy was often made by consensus, within the limits of overall UK budgetary constraints, by rather small groups of people. It was often argued that this made these fields doubly insulated from democratic scrutiny, since there was no Scottish Parliament to hold them responsible, and there was little interest in Scottish matters at Westminster. In other fields, the policy communities were UK-wide, responding to a British rather than a Scottish policy agenda. The main role of the Scottish branches was often to lobby for Scottish interests within their UK body.

Both types of group were challenged by devolution (Keating, Cairney and Hepburn, 2008). Scottish groups are now exposed to more scrutiny from within Scotland and to competition from new actors. UK-based groups are being asked to come up with policy ideas rather than just lobbying. Groups that previously could come together to lobby for Scotland now find themselves competing within the Scottish policy arena, revealing that much of the old talk about consensus was merely due to the fact that they could all agree to gang up on London. Small size may be an advantage when it comes to talking to each other, but it also reveals that they may not always have shared interests. Groups have sometimes struggled to find the resources to staff their Scottish operations and, in some cases, to develop distinctive Scottish policies. The result is that there are still distinct policy communities in some fields such as education and law, although these are challenged by new interests. In other fields, like health, Scottish policy communities are strengthening and policy is consciously diverging from that in England. Elsewhere, as, for example, in industrial relations, Scottish policy communities are under-developed. In the case of independence, then, these fields would be under-institutionalised and new mechanisms for policy-making would have to be put in place.

Scotland's style of policy-making is rather distinct from that of Whitehall as a result of this inheritance. There is a strong commitment to working with representative groups, or 'stakeholders' within policy communities and an emphasis on reaching agreement, in contrast to the bolder and often more confrontational style found in England. The outcome may be that there is less radical change, but change sticks better. We can contrast the frenetic and repeated reorganisations of health and education in England with the more gradual pace of reform in Scotland. Small size undoubtedly plays a role here, as it is possible to gather everyone together to discuss change and to follow it through in detail. There is a widespread belief, however, that while Scotland may have avoided some of the disasters that have afflicted poorly thought-out initiatives at the UK and English levels (such as those documented in King and Crewe, 2013), there has been a lack of policy innovation. In many instances, Scotland's distinctiveness lies in not following England rather than in striking out on its own. Small size and the need to maintain consensus within policy communities may, indeed, militate against radical change.

Scotland's policy style can be seen as a form of social partnership, as governments and representative groups work out policy among themselves but it is a sectoral partnership, within individual policy fields, rather than a broad pattern of social concertation in which compromises are reached. The United Kingdom did experiment with forms of concertation or corporatism in the 1960s and 1970s under both Conservative and Labour governments, as we noted earlier. There was a Scottish Economic Council, which survived the abolition of the Regional Economic Development Councils in England in 1979 but died out in the 1980s. It was not, in any case, a powerful body, given that neither the Scottish Office nor the social partners were able to make real decisions at the Scottish level. Since devolution, there has been no move to establish an Economic and Social Council, which is perhaps surprising given the existence of such councils or equivalent mechanisms in many devolved European regions (Keating,

2013a). As in the rest of the United Kingdom, corporatism still has a bad name in Scotland.

Scotland shares with the rest of the United Kingdom a liberal market form of capitalism focused on individual competing firms and share value. It notably lacks the kind of coordinated market economy of countries where social partnership has thrived. There has been some talk about moving to a more long-term form of business planning, for example in the Common Weal project but this would itself be a long-term process. There has also been talk of building up a tier of medium-sized firms based in Scotland, which might also facilitate social dialogue but again this is a deep structural issue not amenable to immediate policy interventions. Meanwhile, an independent Scotland would inherit existing structures, which might be modified to a greater or lesser degree.

The Scottish Government's independence White Paper did suggest a National Convention of Employment and Labour Relations as a forum for dialogue. The need for such a body was demonstrated in 2013 in the crisis over the Grangemouth industrial complex, when nobody seemed able to bring the sides together in the right place and secure both a compromise settlement to the dispute between unions and the employer, and the broader national interest. As a result, a vital part of Scotland's industrial infrastructure was almost lost. It is not clear, beyond this, what role the new council would have. There seem to be no proposals for a Scottish level of wage bargaining such as exists in corporatist states, which might enable trade unions to bargain over a range of issues, including the 'social wage'.

Indeed, neither unions nor employers have the strong representative organisations at this level, which would be needed. Trade union density in Scotland is slightly higher than the UK average, at about a third of all employees, but this is well below the levels found in the Nordic states (Table 5.1). The Scottish Trades Union Congress has shown some interest in social partnership, especially during Ireland's experiment with it but it cannot bind its member unions. Employers are really not interested at all and their representative bodies are fragmented and rarely able to speak authoritatively, let alone act in a broad business interest. The independence White Paper talks in general terms about 'constructive dialogue' across all economic sectors but not about how this might be institutionalised or the incentives for the social partners to participate. The SNP's proposal to cut corporation tax for all businesses without asking anything whatever in return suggests social partnership would be very much a voluntary idea.

External Relations

An independent Scotland would be a small state on the edge of Europe, caught between competing poles. There is the UK pole, which as Ireland has found, will continue to be important. This to a large extent means England, although the potential for alliances and exchange of experience with Northern Ireland, Wales and, eventually perhaps, English regions, can provide an alternative perspective. There is the European pole, focused on the European Union. There is the North Atlantic pole, dominated by the United States although British governments have insisted, with ever-less plausibility, on a special relationship that allows them a real influence in this sphere. This is not merely a geo-strategic choice or a matter of security policy, but also a choice of social and economic models. Ireland has also been torn between the European and the North Atlantic pole and, after an apparent period of Europhilia, has now become more Atlanticist in its politics and social models. There is a northern European pole, expressed in the Nordic grouping, which has long been a source of inspiration to the SNP.

The independence movement in Scotland is committed to remaining in the European Union, which would secure access to the single market and deliver a range of policies from competition rules to environmental regulation, which a small country would find it difficult to provide for itself. There is really no doubt that Scotland, as a European democracy compliant with the *acquis communautaire* (the EU's body of law and policy) would gain entry (Keating, 2013b). To exclude it would violate the very democratic principles upon which the EU is founded. Nor would it be in anybody's interest to exclude Scotland from the single market, even temporarily. No member state has indicated that it would veto Scotland's membership, although there were repeated suggestions (including from the unionist side in the UK) that somebody else (rarely named) might do so. Such suggestions that Scotland would be left outside the EU are no more than scaremongering.

The more difficult question concerns the terms on which Scotland would enter. The independence White Paper proposed keeping the existing UK opt-outs on the single currency (the Euro), the Schengen zone of

passport-free travel, justice and home affairs, and various social provisions. This might be the simplest thing to do, ensuring the minimum of
disruption, and the UK government would presumably not want to break
up the existing UK single market by introducing restrictions, let alone
establishing border controls with Scotland (as some UK ministers suggested). The result, however, would be to tie Scotland to the UK pole as a
semi-detached EU member rather than a small player at the heart of
Europe. Large EU member states have a big influence over policy, even if
they choose to remain on the periphery. Small states, as we have noted,
need to be more active and to establish their credentials as good Europeans. This suggests that Scotland would be better to enter into core
Europe rather than sit on the sidelines. If the rest of the UK drifts further
away from core Europe, Scotland risks being dragged along behind it,
losing further influence.

Keeping the Pound as the currency of an independent Scotland would
not only limit Scotland's macroeconomic policy options. It would also
complicate relations with Europe, as it moves towards greater economic
coordination and more unified financial regulation. The UK was joined
only by the Czech Republic in refusing to sign up the Treaty on Stability,
Coordination and Governance in 2012. An independent Scotland adopting
the same line would put itself further from the European pole and closer
to the UK one. If the UK were to withdraw from the EU altogether, then
Scotland would be even more exposed. It is difficult to see how it could
continue, as an EU state, to share a currency with a non-member state,
especially as the EU, without the British presence, would likely move to
greater union in financial regulation.

There have been various proposals to keep some kind of UK or Islands
framework to manage common affairs after independence. The example
of the Nordic Council is often cited, as is the British-Irish Council set up
as part of the Northern Ireland settlement. Yet the Nordic Council is a
rather weak body for exchanging ideas and experiences rather than a
decision-making instance. It has further been weakened by the fact that
some of its members are within the EU and others are not. The British-Irish
Council, similarly, does not limit the prerogatives of its member states in
the way that the European Union does. An independent Scotland might
agree to pool its sovereignty in a stronger Council of the Islands in return
for greater influence but it is highly unlikely that the United Kingdom
would do so, since it would get so little in return. The strongest safeguard

for small independent states remains the European Union, which does exercise supranational authority and in which large states are constrained.

Telling the Story

Scotland is not a 'homogeneous' society in the sense meant by Alesina and Spoloare (2013) but, like other small nations, it sustains a series of stories about itself, which can underpin policy trajectories. Nations, as we noted earlier, are embedded in cultures in the form of myths, symbols and self-understandings. These provide perspectives for appraising social and political choices and bases for collective action. Myths are not, contrary to common understanding, necessarily wrong. Their power depends on their being believed, whether right, wrong or, most likely, partly right. Scotland is in no way unusual in sustaining a series of myths about the nation and its history. As the notoriously anti-Scottish historian Hugh Trevor-Roper (2008) admitted in his last (posthumous) book, it is perhaps the English who are the exception in not continually revising and re-inventing their own history.

Where Scotland is perhaps most distinct is in the co-existence of contrasting myths and contested views of the nation. The 'Caledonian antisysygy' (Smith 1919) draws on a persistent Manichean tradition of the clash of opposites. There is a long-standing critique of clichéd images of the country, including what Tom Nairn once called the 'tartan monster' and the kailyard school of literature. In recent decades nationalists have consciously promoted a multicultural vision of the nation, at the polar opposite from Alesina and Spoloare's fantasies about ethnic homogeneity. The idea that, for Scotland to exist, it must be 'different' in some essentialised way has been laid to rest. Political autonomy has allowed it to define membership of the community in an inclusive manner as a form of civic citizenship rather than by ancestry. Visions of the nation have also been recast, by politicians of all perspectives, away from a romanticised past and towards a more modern, progressive and forward-looking outlook. Red Clydeside remains a strong myth for the Scottish left but has less resonance now than it did in the 1970s. Devolution, by providing an authoritative political forum and opening up debate, has itself made the nation less reliant on the clichéd visions of the past.

Yet essentialised visions of the nation do persist. One example is the idea that Scots lack self-confidence (Craig, 2003), a stereotype that has never actually been measured scientifically or compared with other nations. There was a story about secular economic decline popularised in the years after devolution, even while Scotland was catching up with the wealthier parts of the United Kingdom. There is a myth of egalitarianism, in defiance of the evidence of massive inequalities, although this has been so thoroughly criticised that the counter-myth may be more powerful. In recent decades, Scotland has been reconstituted as a political community and an arena for public policy making but the fear of falling back into the old stereotypes has inhibited the development of new visions for the nation and its place in the world.

It is possible that independence itself could provide the shock that would shift old practices and attitudes. As an independent state, Scotland could worry less about nationality and defining the nation and could be forced into new forms of social cooperation. Alternatively, cooperation could be a learning process in which institutional reforms gradually changed attitudes and relationships. This would not in itself, however, allow it to escape some of the essential choices that must be made about policy and institutions.

Is Independence Necessary?

In this book, we have compared Scotland with small independent nations but the long-term choices cannot be reduced to independence or union. Independence as offered by the SNP is highly attenuated, notably by continuation of monetary union with the United Kingdom. The unionist parties insist that further change is possible within the union. The main items that are not currently devolved are the welfare state in the form of cash transfers, and taxation. With more of these devolved it might be that a social investment state is attainable within the United Kingdom.

The current allocation of powers in social welfare is largely inherited from the old Scottish Office system, but is consistent with traditional federal and public goods theories. Redistributive matters are mostly reserved for the centre, as are the main macroeconomic powers while allocative matters such as the organisation of public services, are largely devolved. This was also true of the devolution proposals of the 1970s, with the exception that the current settlement gives Scotland some important instruments in the field of economic development. There are two rationales for reserving redistributive powers. First is an instrumental argument, that a larger area is better able to mobilise resources for redistribution and insure against asymmetric shocks. Second is the argument that it is at the level of the nation that affective solidarity exists, which provides the rationale for selecting the community within which redistribution takes place – no welfare states are ever truly universal. These arguments were recently explicitly confirmed in the Calman report (Commission on Scottish Devolution (2008) and the later report of the Scottish Labour Party (2014). These assumptions must, at least, be modified in the current era of welfare state transformation. There are two dimensions here, the functional and the territorial.

Social policy specialists talk of old and new social risks. Old social risks are those posed by the traditional industrial labour market and male-headed household. They include the need for family support, pensions and insurance against spells of unemployment. New social risks reflect the complexities of modern society. They include the highly complex mechanisms of generation and reproduction of poverty, about which there is little consensus; skill erosion in a high-tech economy; changing family structures; precarious employment; and new demographic challenges. The context also includes the appreciation that generational and gender divisions are also relevant. There is a broad consensus on the need to move from passive support to active measures to incorporate excluded sections of the population in the labour market, although there are striking differences between right and left on the generation of the new inequalities and on how they should be tackled, notably on the balance between incentives and coercion. The modern vocabulary includes 'social inclusion', 'activation', 'social investment', 'active labour market policy' and 'workfare'.

The old distinction between redistributive and allocative policies has also broken down, with the appreciation that most policies (and all public services) are redistributive to some degree. This is especially true if we enlarge the notion of distribution beyond income groups to include things like gender, generation and place.

On the territorial dimension, recent years have seen a rescaling of functional systems across economic, social and cultural domains, and a rescaling of government to match (Keating, 2013a). The 'new regionalism' literature emphasises the way in which economic restructuring follows global, regional and local logics, and not just national ones (Keating, 1998). Regions and cities have been identified as key levels for the analysis of economic and social restructuring and the emergence of new problems and policy opportunities. Training and active labour market policies are increasingly elaborated and implemented at local and regional levels, corresponding to labour markets. Politics at these levels is increasingly contested by social forces seeking to define the terms of development projects, notably the balance between competitive growth, social inclusion and environmental considerations. The idea of inter-regional competition within open markets has become a central feature of political debate, although it has been questioned in economic theory.

At the same time, national solidarity is under challenge as affective identities are shifting. The evidence here is mixed and rather inconsistent, but it is at least no longer axiomatic that the nation state is the sole locus of social solidarity, especially in plurinational states. There is evidence of welfare differentiation across devolved regions in Europe, largely in the form of differing definitions of the deserving target groups and more in the field of services than of cash payments.

There is a strong argument for Europeanising certain welfare provisions. Europe is now the framework for market regulation and therefore for its social counterpart. It is Europe, not the nation state, that covers the largest population and most resources and can best respond to asymmetrical shocks. On the other hand, it is manifestly clear that Europe has not generated the affective solidarity to make it possible to produce more than small-scale transfers through Cohesion policy, and one-off bailouts.

All of this is prising apart the formally coterminous domains of economic regulation, social solidarity, political representation and governing institutions. It does not mean that solidarity is leaving the nation state and relocating at either the supranational or substate level. We are witnessing, rather, a multilevel solidarity, operating at distinct scales and in different arenas. The old assumptions no longer apply.

In present-day Scotland these functional and territorial dimensions intersect, shaping the discussion of social welfare and devolution. Survey evidence shows that Scots do not differ radically from citizens elsewhere in the United Kingdom in their broad preferences for welfare. Public policy, however, does not emerge directly from citizen preferences but from the aggregation and compromise among interests and preferences within political institutions. This has produced a rather different balance within Scotland, notably on matters of universalism and public provision. In the longer term, such differences necessarily imply distinct fiscal choices, and indicate the need for mechanisms by which Scotland might recapture the benefits of its own social investments, for example in university education or childcare. It also points to changes in the balance of welfare instruments so as to fit local needs and preferences. Measures like the 'bedroom tax/ spare room subsidy', designed for conditions in the south of England, may have little relevance in Scotland (or in the north of England for that matter).

As a matter of functional efficiency, the present division between passive welfare (reserved) and active welfare (largely devolved) creates mismatches and disincentives, which are beginning to be recognised. The location of housing benefit and social housing at different levels is one instance. Another matter is the interface among unemployment support and disability support with training, economic development, urban regeneration and social work services. There is never an undisputed optimal level for the integration of public services and the idea of 'joined-up government' is often a naïve illusion, but we can probably do a lot better than at present.

It is fruitless to design a reformed system of devolution predicated on the present mode of welfare state. One thing that we do know is that the welfare state is going to undergo some major changes, if only for pressing financial reasons. This provides an opportunity to rethink how Scottish welfare might fit into an emerging multilevel model and how resources might most effectively be deployed.

The case of Quebec is exemplary here. After independence was rejected in two referendums (very narrowly in the second instance in 1995), Quebec parked the constitutional issue for a long time. It continued, however, to build the nation and develop its institutions. It was once seen as a somewhat corporatist developmental state, with a model of social partnership referred to as 'Quebec Inc.'. It was also seen as rather more social democratic than other parts of Canada and certainly than the United States. As in the Nordic countries, much of the formal apparatus of corporatism has disappeared in the face of neo-liberalism and market capitalism. Yet there remains a culture of cooperation such that the response to crisis often takes the form of 'summits' of key actors. There is still a shared commitment to Quebec as a political and economic community and the main frame of reference for public debates. Quebec has a very distinct attitude to childcare, anticipating many of the policies in the Scottish Government's White Paper which, as critics have noted, could be enacted within the existing devolution settlement. It has sustained a larger public sector, more social spending and slightly higher taxes than neighbouring jurisdictions.

The result is that, while social inequality has been increasing in the rest of Canada and converging on that in the United States, Quebec has resisted the trend (Noël, 2013).

After the Referendum

The outcome of the 2014 referendum on Scottish independence demonstrated three things. First, there was no majority for independence. Second, a substantial minority (45 per cent) of the voters did opt for independence, a higher number than had normally been found in opinion polls over the years. Third, a large number of people favoured more powers for Scotland within the union. Arguably, we knew all this already but the result did demonstrate rather definitively the absence of majorities for either independence or union as either of these have normally been seen. What was less predictable was the massive engagement of the citizenry in the referendum debate and the way that this focused not on abstract notions of independence, but on precisely the social and economic questions addressed in this book. Scotland matured as a political community and became a primary point of reference for debates about economy and welfare and the trade-offs that might be made between the two. These issues have not been settled but remain at the centre of politics, now entwined with the issue of Scottish self-government and the possibility of a distinct Scottish economic and social model.

It is one of the ironies of the referendum campaign that, having insisted that the choice was between independence and union and that no 'third way' should feature on the ballot, the unionist parties declared in the last week that a No vote would now be taken as a mandate for more devolution; this was the famous 'vow'. This might have presaged a convergence between the two sides on a package of measures that would have allowed Scotland the powers to achieve what Quebec has done. Such a convergence has not, however, occurred. The unionist vow promised a very rapid timetable for change and, after the referendum, gave birth to the interparty Smith Commission, with a mandate to produce proposals by St Andrew's Day (30 November) 2014 and draft legislation by Burns Night (25 January) 2015. This was not enough time for a mature debate comparable to that which had taken place over independence, or for the technical work needed to ensure that the package was coherent and workable. The nationalists, boosted by their respectable performance in the referendum, asked for all domestic powers (and accepted whatever they were given) rather than focusing on the strategic competences needed to fashion a Scottish social model. The unionists conceded powers in a rather piecemeal fashion rather than thinking of broad and coherent blocks of instruments.

The powers envisaged by the Smith report mainly concern taxation and welfare. Scotland would gain substantial revenues, notably the whole of income tax on earned income, and half of Value Added Tax. It could alter the bands and rates of income tax although not the threshold for paying tax. VAT revenues would be assigned, without the Scottish Parliament being able to alter the rates; EU law does not allow the latter. On the welfare side, Universal Credit would remain a UK-wide benefit (with some small exceptions), which would exclude the possibility of better matching benefit levels to development priorities. There would be some administrative devolution in active labour market policy, but not a capacity to shape the policy itself. This is not broad enough to allow Scotland to pursue its own policies along Nordic or even Quebec lines.

On the other hand, the referendum and its aftermath have focused attention on what Scotland can do with its existing powers with even modest additions. When the SNP promised extended child care in its independence White Paper, its opponents noted that it could do this under existing powers. The SNP response that they would not gain the tax revenues from the additional employment now falls if it is the Scottish Parliament that receives all income tax. The SNP have abandoned their policy of cutting corporation tax indiscriminately in favour of selected allowances for firms pursuing particular objectives; this resembles the Basque approach. In turn, this opens the possibility of social dialogue and partnership, with business and government making mutual concessions and contributions. The main parties in Scotland remain open to this form of policy making and the social partners may now be more amenable. There is a broad consensus on the desirability of less social inequality, more long-term thinking and a social investment approach.

In the Centre on Constitutional Change, we are now working on these possibilities, identifying challenges for Scotland in taxation, social inequality, the future of welfare and institutions for policy making. The independence debate may be over (at least for the time being) but the challenges of being a small state in a big world are not. There is a tendency in Scotland to act as though it was the only small country in this situation but this is a larger issue, going to the heart of the European system of nation states and the future of Europe itself. That is another issue that we will continue to follow.

Glossary

Corporatism	Corporatism is the making of economic and social policy by negotiation among government, employers and trade unions.
Keynesian	Keynesianism is an economic philosophy named after British economist John Maynard Keynes (1883–1946). Keynesians believe in using taxation and public expenditure to regulate overall demand and smooth out booms and recessions.
Macroeconomic	Macroeconomics refers to the broad economic factors influencing growth. The principal tools of macroeconomic policy are fiscal (taxes and spending) and monetary (interest rates, credit and money supply). Macroeconomic policy can be contrasted with microeconomic, which refers to industrial policy, research and development and individual sectors of the economy.
Market liberal	A market liberal believes in minimal government intervention in the economy.
Neo-liberalism	Neo-liberalism is a term applied (often in a derogatory sense) to market liberalism.
Protectionism	Protectionism refers to policies seeking to reduce competition by sheltering domestic industries from foreign rivals, or sustaining sectors that are uncompetitive.
Reflation	Reflation is the use of fiscal (tax and spending) policies to increase demand in the economy. It is the standard Keynesian response to recession.
Social concertation	Social concertation is a looser form of corporatism, in which employers and trade unions, sometimes along with government, agree about policy priorities.

Social investment

Social investment is public expenditure aimed at improving the productive economy.

Tripartite bargaining

Tripartite bargaining refers to the role of employers, trades unions and government in corporatism or social concertation.

References

Agius, Christine (2007), 'Sweden's 2006 Parliamentary Election and After: Contesting or Consolidating the Swedish Model' in *Parliamentary Affairs*, 60.4: 585–600.

Aidukaite, Jolanta (2006), 'The formation of social insurance institutions of the Baltic States in the post-socialist era' in *Journal of European Social Policy*, 16.3: 259–270.

Aidukaite, Jolanta (2009), 'Old welfare state theories and new welfare regimes in Eastern Europe: Challenges and implications' in *Communist and Post-Communist Studies*, 42: 23–39.

Alesina, Alberto and Enrico Spoloare (2003), *The Size of Nations*, Cambridge, Mass.: MIT Press.

Allern, Elin Haugsgjerd (2010), 'Survival of a Majority Coalition: The Norwegian Parliamentary Election of 14 September 2009' in *West European Politics*, 33.4: 904–912.

Armstrong, Angus and Monique Ebell (2013), 'Scotland's Currency Options', London: National Institute of Economic and Social Research.

Avdagic, Sabina, Martin Rhodes and Jelle Visser (2011), *Social Pacts in Europe: Emergence, Evolution and Institutionalization*, Oxford: Oxford University Press.

Aylott, Nicholas and Niklas Bolin (2007), 'Towards a Two-Party System? The Swedish Parliamentary Election of September 2006' in *West European Politics*, 30.3: 621–633.

Banfield, Edward C. (1958), *The Moral Basis of a Backward Society*, New York: The Free Press.

Bell, David and David Eiser (2014), *Inequality in Scotland: Trends, Drivers, and Implications for the Independence Debate*, Edinburgh: ESRC Scottish Centre on Constitutional Change.

Bohle, Dorothee and Béla Greskovits (2013), *Capitalist Diversity on Europe's Periphery*, Ithaca: Cornell University Press.

Brandal, Nik., Øivind Bratberg and Dag Einar Thorsen (2013) *The Nordic Model of Social Democracy*, Basingstoke: Palgrave Macmillan.

Calmfors, Lars (1993), 'Lessons from the Macroeconomic Experience of Sweden' in *European Journal of Political Economy*, 9.1: 25–72.

Christiansen, Neils Finn and Pirjo Markkola (2006), 'Introduction' in Christiansen, Neils Finn, Klaus Petersen, Nils Edling and Per Haave. (eds) *The Nordic Model of Welfare: A Historical Reappraisal*, Copenhagen: Museum Tusculanum Press.

Cichon, Michael (1999), 'Notional Defined-contribution Schemes: Old Wine in New Bottles?' in *International Social Security Review*, 52.4: 87–105.

Compston, Hugh (2002), 'The Strange Persistence of Policy Concertation', in Stefan Berger and Hugh Compston (eds), *Policy Concertation and Social Partnership in Western Europe*, Oxford: Berghahn.

Commission on Scottish Devolution (Calman Commission) (2008), *The Future of Scottish Devolution within the Union: A First Report*, presented to the Presiding Officer of the Scottish Parliament and to the Secretary of State for Scotland, on behalf of Her Majesty's Government.

Craig, Carol (2003), *The Scots' Crisis of Self-Confidence*, Glasgow: Big Thinking.

Crouch, Colin (2013), 'Class Politics and the Social Investment Welfare State', in Michael Keating and David McCrone (eds), *The Crisis of Social Democracy in Europe*, Edinburgh: Edinburgh University Press.

Curtice, John (2013), *What Does England Want?*, Edinburgh: Scottish Centre for Social Research.

Curtice, John and Oliver Heath (2009), 'Do people want choice and diversity of provision in public services?' in Alison Park, John Curtice, Katarina Thomson, Miranda Philips and Elizabeth Clery (eds), British Social Attitudes: The 25th Report, London: Sage.

Curtice, John and Rachel Ormiston (2011), *Is Scotland more left-wing than England?*, Edinburgh: Scottish Centre for Social Research.

Dahrendorf, Ralph (1995), 'Preserving Prosperity', *New Statesman and Society*, 13.29: 36–40.

Dellepiane, Sebastian and Niamh Hardiman (2012), 'Governing the

Irish Economy: A triple crisis', in Niamh Hardiman (ed.), *Irish Governance in Crisis*, Manchester: Manchester University Press.

Dølvik, Jon Erik, 'The Nordic regimes of labour market governance: From crisis to success-story?' in *Fafos Rådsprogram 2006–2008*, Fafo-paper 2007:07.

Eamets, Raul and Epp Kallaste (2004) 'The Role of Trade Unions in Labour Market Flexibility: The Case of Estonia', Papers presented in a research seminar on the labour market, Tallinn, Estonia, 9 May 2003, pp. 39–58 online at: http://www.eestipank.info/ pub/ en/dokumendid/publikatsioonid/seeriad/konverentsid/_20030509/ _2.pdf

Eirtheim, P. and Kuhnle, S. (2000), 'Nordic Welfare States in the 1990s: Institutional Stability, Signs of Divergence', in Stein Kuhnle (ed.), *Survival of the European Welfare State*, Routledge/ECPR Studies in European Political Science, New York: Routledge.

Elschner, Christina and Verner Vanborren (2009), *Corporate Effective Tax Rates in an Enlarged European Union*, Brussels: European Commission.

Engels Friedrich (1849), 'The Magyar Struggle' *Neue Rheinische Zeitung* (13 January 1849).

Esping-Andersen, Gøsta, (1996), *Welfare States in Transition: National Adaptations in Global Economies*, London: Sage Publications.

Ferguson, Yale H. and Richard W. Mansbach (1996), *Polities: Authority, Identities, and Change*, Columbia: University of South Carolina Press.

Fukuyama, Francis (1992), *The End of History and the Last Man*, New York: Free Press.

Gardham, Magnus (2012), 'Russell: I was wrong on universal benefits', *The Herald*, 3 October.

Guéhenno, Jean-Marie (1993), *La fin de la démocratie*, Paris: Flammarion.

Guéhenno, Jean-Marie (2000), *The End of the Nation-state*, University of Minnesota Press.

Hall, Peter A. and David Soskice (2001), 'An Introduction to Varieties of Capitalism', in Peter A. Hall and David Soskice (eds), *Varieties of*

Capitalism: The Institutional Foundations of Comparative Advantage, Oxford: Oxford University Press.

Haughton, Jonathan (2005), 'Growth in Output and Living Standards' in J. O'Hagan and C. Newman (eds), *The Economy of Ireland. National and Sectoral Policy Issues*, 9th edition, Dublin: Gill and Macmillan, 2005.

Helliwell, John, Richard Layard and Jeffery Sachs (2013), *World Happiness Report 2013*, New York: United Nations.

Hemerijck, Anton (2013), *Changing Welfare States*, Oxford: Oxford University Press.

Hilson, Mary (2008) *The Nordic Model: Scandinavia Since 1945*, London: Reaktion Books Ltd.

Hobsbawm, Eric (1990), *Nations and Nationalism since 1780: Programme, Myth, Reality*, Cambridge: Cambridge University Press.

Honkapohja, Seppo and Erkki Koskela (1999), 'The Economic Crisis of the 1990s in Finland' in *Economic Policy*, 14.29: 399–436.

Jensen, Nathan M. (2012), 'Fiscal Policy and the Firm: Do Low Corporate Tax Rates Attract Multinational Corporations?' in *Comparative Political Studies* 45: 1004–1026.

Jimmy Reid Foundation (2013), *The Common Weal: A Model for Economic and Social Development in Scotland*, Glasgow: Jimmy Reid Foundation.

Johnston, Tom (1952), *Memories*, Glasgow: Collins.

Jones, Erik (2008), *Economic Adjustment and Political Transformation in Small States*, Oxford: Oxford University Press.

Jonung, Lars (2008), 'Lessons from Financial Liberalisation in Scandinavia' in *Comparative Economic Studies*, 50.4: 564–598.

Jørgensen, Henning, (2000), 'Danish labour market policy since 1994 – the new 'Columbus' egg' of labour market regulation?' in P. Klemmer and R. Wink (eds.) *Preventing Unemployment in Europe*, Ruhr Research Institute for Regional and Innovation Policy, Cheltenham: Edward Elgar.

Jørgensen, Henning and Michaela Schulze, (2011), 'Leaving the Nordic Path? The Changing Role of Danish Trade Unions in the Welfare Reform Process' in *Social Policy & Administration*, 45.2: 206–219.

Kangas, Olli and Joakim Palme (2009), 'Making social policy work for economic development: the Nordic experience' in *International Journal of Social Welfare*, 18: 62–72.

Kangas, Olli and Joakim Palme (2005), 'Coming Late – Catching Up: The Formation of a "Nordic Model"' in Kangas, Olli and Joakim Palme (eds.) (2005), *Social Policy and Economic Development in the Nordic Countries*, Basingstoke: Palgrave Macmillan.

Katzenstein, Peter J. (1985), *Small States in World Markets: Industrial Policy in Europe*, Ithaca: Cornell University Press.

Kautto, Mikko, Johann Fritzell, et. al. (eds.) (2005), *Nordic Welfare States in the European Context*, London: Routledge.

Keating, Michael (1998), *The New Regionalism in Western Europe. Territorial Restructuring and Political Change*, Cheltenham: Edward Elgar.

Keating, Michael (2008), 'Culture and social science', in Donatella della Porta and Michael Keating (eds.), *Approaches and Methodologies in the Social Sciences: A Pluralist Perspective*, Cambridge: Cambridge University Press.

Keating, Michael (2010), *The Government of Scotland: Public Policy Making after Devolution*, 2nd edn., Edinburgh: Edinburgh University Press.

Keating, Michael (2013a), *Rescaling the European State: The Making of Territory and the Rise of the Meso*, Oxford: Oxford University Press.

Keating, Michael (2013b), 'Scotland and the EU after Independence', http://www.futureukandscotland.ac.uk/papers.

Keating, Michael, Paul Cairney and Eve Hepburn (2008) 'Territorial Policy Communities and Devolution in the United Kingdom', *Cambridge Journal of Regions, Economy and Society* 2.1: 51–66.

Keating, Michael, John Loughlin and Kris Deschouwer (2003), *Culture, Institutions and Economic Development*, Cheltenham: Edward Elgar.

Kettunen, Pauli and Klaus Peterson (2011), *Beyond Welfare State Models: Transnational, Historical Perspectives on Social Policy*, Cheltenham: Edward Elgar.

Kiander J. (2005), 'Growth and employment in the Nordic welfare state in the 1990s: Crisis and revival' in Kangas O, and Palme J, (eds.), *Social policy and Economic Development in the Nordic countries*, Basingstoke: Palgrave-Macmillan/UNRISD.

Kildal, Nanna and Stein Kuhnle (eds.) (2005), *Normative Foundations of the Welfare State: The Nordic Experience*, Abington: Routledge.

King, Anthony and Ivor Crewe (2013), *The Blunders of our Governments*, London: One World.

Kirby, Peader and Mary P. Murphy (2011), *Towards a Second Republic. Irish Politics after the Celtic Tiger*, London: Pluto.

Laar, Mart (1996) 'Estonia's Success Story' in *Journal of Democracy*, 7.1: 96–101.

Lee, J. J. (1989) *Ireland, 1912–1985. Politics and Society*, Cambridge: Cambridge Univeristy Press.

MacLeod, Dennis and Michael Russell (2006), *Grasping the Thistle: How Scotland Must React to the Three Key Challenges of the Twenty First Century*, Glendaruel: Argyll Publishing.

Macwhirter, Iain (2006), 'A Tale of Two Books', *Scottish Review of Books*, 2.4.

McCrone, David (2001), *Understanding Scotland. The Sociology of a Nation*, 2nd edition, London: Routledge.

Madeley, John, T. S. (2002), 'Outside the Whale: Norway's Storting Election of 10 September 2001' in *West European Politics*, 25.2: 212–222.

Marshall, T. H. (1992), *Citizenship and social class*, London: Pluto.

Marklund, Steffan and Anders Nordlund (1999), 'Economic problems, welfare convergence and political instability' in Kauto, Mikko et. al. (eds.) *Nordic Social Policy: Changing Welfare States*, London: Routledge.

Maxwell, Stephen (2013), *Arguing for Independence: Evidence, Risk and the Wicked Issues*, Edinburgh: Luath.

Maxwell, Stephen (201), *The Case for Left-wing Nationalism*, Edinburgh: Luath.

McCrone, Gavin (2013), *Scottish Independence: Weighing up the Economics*, Edinburgh: Birlinn.

Mill, John Stuart (1972), *On Liberty, Utilitarianism, and Considerations on Representative Government*, London: Dent.

Milner, Henry (2013), 'Can the Swedish social model survive the decline of the social democrats?' in Michael Keating and David McCrone (eds.), *The Crisis of Social Democracy in Europe*, Edinburgh: Edinburgh University Press.

Monteith, Brian (2012), 'Ruth Davidson is not Annabel Goldie', Think Scotland, 21 October.

Müller, Katharina (2002), 'Old-Age Security in the Baltics: Legacy, Early Reforms and Recent Trends' in *Europe-Asia Studies*, 54.5: 725–48.

National Economic and Social Council (2013), online at: www.nesc.ie/en/our-organisation/about-nesc/.

NESC (2005), National Economic and Social Council, *The Developmental Welfare State*, Dublin: NESC.

Noël, Alain (2013), 'Quebec's New Politics of Redistribution', in Keith Banting and John Myles (eds.), *The Fading of Redistributive Politics: Policy Change and Policy Drift in Canada*, Vancouver: University of British Columbia Press.

O'Donnell, Rory, Maura Adshead and Damian Thomas (2011), 'Ireland: Two Trajectories of Institutionalization', in Sabina Avdagic, Martin Rhodes and Jelle Visser (2011), *Social Pacts in Europe. Emergence, Evolution and Institutionalization*, Oxford: Oxford University Press.

OECD (2012), 'Income inequality and growth: The role of taxes and transfers', OECD Economics Department Policy Notes No. 9, Paris: OECD.

OECD (2013), 'Country statistical profiles', *Country Statistical Profiles: Key Tables from OECD*, online at: http://www.oecd-ilibrary.org/economics/country-statistical-profiles-key-tables-from-oecd_20752288.

Østrup, Finn, Lars Oxelheim and Clas Wihlborg (2009), 'Origins and Resolution of Financial Crises: Lessons from the Current and Northern European Crises' in *Asian Economic Papers*, 8.3: 178–220.

Ostry, Jonathan D., Andrew Berg, and Charalambos G. Tsangarides (2014), *Redistribution, Inequality, and Growth*, IMF Staff Discussion Note 14/02, Washington: International Monetary Fund.

Panke, Diana (2010), *Small States in the European Union: Coping with Structural Disadvantages*, London: Ashgate.

Paterson, Lindsay, Frank Bechhofer and David McCrone (2004), *Living in Scotland: Social and Economic Change since 1980*, Edinburgh: Edinburgh University Press.

Petersen, Klaus and Klas Åmark (2006), 'Old Age Pensions in the Nordic Countries 1800–2000' in Christiansen, Neils Finn, Klaus Petersen, Nils Edling and Per Haave. (eds.) *The Nordic Model of Welfare: A Historical Reappraisal*, Copenhagen: Museum Tusculanum Press.

Peterson, Christer, (2009), 'The Demise of the Swedish Model and the Coming of Innovative Localities?' in Kristensen, Peer Hull and Kari Lilja (eds.) *New Modes of Globalising: Experimentalist Forms of Economic Organization and Enabling Welfare Institutions – Lessons from the Nordic Countries and Slovenia* (Final Report of the 'Transnational learning through local experimenting' EU 6th Framework programme) Copenhagen and Helsinki.

Porter, Michael (1990), *The Competitive Advantage of Nations*, Basingstoke: Macmillan.

Qvortrup, Mads (2002), 'The Emperor's New Clothes: The Danish General Election 20 November 2001' in *West European Politics*, 25.2: 205–11.

Rajevska, Feliciana (2005), *Social Policy in Latvia: Welfare State under Double pressure*, FAFO Report 498: Project 'Poverty, social assistance and social inclusion – Developments in Estonia and Latvia in a comparative perspective'.

Raudla, Ringa and Rainer Kattel (2011), 'Why did Estonia Choose Fiscal Retrenchment after the 2008 Crisis?' in *Journal of Public Policy*, 31.2: 163–186.

Rhodes, Martin (2001), 'The Political Economy of Social Pacts: "Competitive Corporatism" and European Welfare Reform', in Paul Pierson (ed.), *The New Politics of the Welfare State*, Oxford: Oxford University Press.

Rhodes, Martin (2013), 'Labour Markets, Welfare States and the Dilemmas of European Social Democracy', in Michael Keating and David McCrone (eds.), *The Crisis of Social Democracy in Europe*, Edinburgh: Edinburgh University Press.

Rodrik, Dani (1998), 'Why do more open economies have bigger governments?' in Journal of Political Economy, 106.5: 997–1032.

Rokkan, Stein (1999), *State Formation, Nation-Building and Mass Politics in Europe. The Theory of Stein Rokkan* edited by Peter Flora, Stein Kuhnle and Derek Urwin, Oxford: Oxford University Press.

Rosie, Michael and Ross Bond (2007), 'Social Democratic Scotland?' in Michael Keating (ed.), Scottish Social Democracy, Brussels: Presses Interuniversitaires Européennes/Peter Lang.

Sabel, Charles F. (1993), 'Studied Trust: Building New Forms of Cooperation in a Volatile Economy', *Human Relations*, 46.9: 1133–70.

Schmitter, Philippe (1974), 'Still the Century of Corporatism?', *The Review of Politics*, 36.1: 85–131.

Scottish Government (2013), *Scotland's Future: Your Guide to an Independent Scotland*, Edinburgh: Scottish Government.

Scottish Labour Party (2014), *Powers for a Purpose: Strengthening Accountability and Empowering People*, Glasgow: Scottish Labour Devolution Commission.

SCVO (2012), *A better state: inclusive principles for Scottish welfare*, Edinburgh: Scottish Council of Voluntary Organisations.

Sitter, Nick (2006) 'Norway's Storting Election of September 2005: Back to the Left' in West European Politics, 29.3: 573–580.

Skilling, David (2012), In Uncertain Seas: Positioning Small Countries to Succeed in a Changing World, Singapore: Landfall Strategy Group.

Smith, G. Gregory (1919), *Scottish Literature: Character and Influence*, London: Macmillan.

Spruyt, Hendrik (1994), *The Sovereign State and its Competitors: An Analysis of Systems Change*, Princeton: Princeton University Press.

Steinberg, Jonathan (1996), *Why Switzerland?*, 2nd edn., Cambridge: Cambridge University Press.

Stephens, John, D. (1996) 'The Scandinavian Welfare State: Achievements, Crisis and Prospects' in Gøsta Esping-Andersen, (ed.) *Welfare States in Transition: National Adaptations in Global Economies*, London: Sage Publications.

Stiglitz, Joseph (2012), *The Price of Inequality*, London: Penguin.

STUC (2013), *A Just Scotland*, Glasgow: Scottish Trades Union Congress.

Thorhallsson, Baldur and Rainer Kattel (2012) 'Neo-Liberal Small States and Economic Crisis: Lessons for Democratic Corporatism' in *Journal of Baltic Studies*, 44.1: 83–103.

Traxler, Franz (2004), 'The metamorphoses of corporatism: From classical to lean patterns', in *European Journal of Political Research*, 43.4: 571–98.

Trevor-Roper, Hugh (2008) *The Invention of Scotland: Myth and History*, edited by Jeremy J. Cater. New Haven: Yale University Press.

Vilpišauskas, Ramūnas (2014) 'Lithuania's double transition after the re-establishment of independence in 1990: coping with uncertainty domestically and externally' in *Oxford Review of Economic Policy*, (Special Issue: Small Country Independence) 30.1.

Weiler, Joseph (2013), 'Editorial', in *European Journal of International Law*, 24.4: 909–13.

Wilkinson, Richard and Kate Pickett (2010), *The Spirit Level: Why Equality is Better for Everyone*, Harmondsworth: Penguin.

World Bank (2013), World Development Indicators: Distribution of income or consumption, data collated online at: http://wdi.worldbank.org/table/2.9

Some other books published by **LUATH** PRESS

Blossom: What Scotland Needs to Flourish

Lesley Riddoch
ISBN: 978-1-908373-69-4 PBK £11.99

 Weeding out vital components of Scottish identity from decades of political and social tangle is no mean task, but it's one journalist Lesley Riddoch has undertaken.

Dispensing with the tired, yo-yoing jousts over fiscal commissions, devo something-or-other and EU in-or-out, *Blossom* pinpoints both the buds of growth and the blight that's holding Scotland back. Drawing from its people and history, as well as the experience of the Nordic countries and the author's own passionate and outspoken perspective, this is a plain-speaking but incisive call to restore equality and control to local communities and let Scotland flourish.

Not so much an intervention in the independence debate as a heartfelt manifesto for a better democracy.
THE SCOTSMAN

A hard-hitting condition of Scotland tour-de-force and a characteristically feisty contribution to (and beyond) the present constitutional debate.
PADDY BORT, Product Magazine

Caledonian Dreaming: The Quest for a Different Scotland

Gerry Hassan
ISBN: 978-1-910021-32-3 PBK £11.99

 *Caledonian Dreaming: The Quest for a Different Scotland* offers a penetrating and original way forward for Scotland beyond the current independence debate.

It identifies the myths of modern Scotland, describes what they say and why they need to be seen as myths. Hassan argues that Scotland is already changing, as traditional institutions and power decline and new forces emerge, and outlines a prospectus for Scotland to become more democratic and to embrace radical and far-reaching change.

With one bound Scotland could be free! How tempting that looks to the progressive-minded on both sides of the border. If only it were that easy, Gerry Hassan drills down to deeper reasons why the many dysfunctions of British democracy could dog an independent Scotland too. With a non-partisan but beady eye on society both sides of the border, in this clever book here are tougher questions to consider than a mere Yes/No.

POLLY TOYNBEE, writer and journalist, The Guardian

Details of this and other books published by Luath Press can be found at:
www.luath.co.uk

Luath Press Limited

committed to publishing well written books worth reading

LUATH PRESS takes its name from Robert Burns, whose little collie Luath (*Gael.*, swift or nimble) tripped up Jean Armour at a wedding and gave him the chance to speak to the woman who was to be his wife and the abiding love of his life. Burns called one of 'The Twa Dogs' Luath after Cuchullin's hunting dog in Ossian's *Fingal*. Luath Press was established in 1981 in the heart of Burns country, and now resides a few steps up the road from Burns' first lodgings on Edinburgh's Royal Mile.

Luath offers you distinctive writing with a hint of unexpected pleasures.

Most bookshops in the UK, the US, Canada, Australia, New Zealand and parts of Europe either carry our books in stock or can order them for you. To order direct from us, please send a £sterling cheque, postal order, international money order or your credit card details (number, address of cardholder and expiry date) to us at the address below. Please add post and packing as follows: UK – £1.00 per delivery address; overseas surface mail – £2.50 per delivery address; overseas airmail – £3.50 for the first book to each delivery address, plus £1.00 for each additional book by airmail to the same address. If your order is a gift, we will happily enclose your card or message at no extra charge.

ILLUSTRATION: IAN KELLAS

Luath Press Limited
543/2 Castlehill
The Royal Mile
Edinburgh EH1 2ND
Scotland

Telephone: 0131 225 4326 (24 hours)
Fax: 0131 225 4324
email: sales@luath.co.uk
Website: www.luath.co.uk